Queer Representation in Literature and Popular Culture

Edited by

Dhishna Pannikot

National Institute of Technology Karnataka

and

Tanupriya

CHRIST (Deemed to be University), Delhi NCR

Series in Critical Media Studies

VERNON PRESS

www.vernonpress.com

In the Americas:
Vernon Press
1000 N West Street, Suite 1200,
Wilmington, Delaware 19801
United States

In the rest of the world:
Vernon Press
C/Sancti Espiritu 17,
Malaga, 29006
Spain

Series in Critical Media Studies

Library of Congress Control Number: 2025935443

Digital Object Identifier (DOI): 10.54094/b-3eb44ec0ac

ISBN: 979-8-8819-0351-0
Also available: 979-8-8819-0286-5 [Hardback]; 979-8-8819-0350-3 [PDF, E-Book]

Cover design by Vernon Press. Background image by jcomp on Freepik.

Contents

Preface

Dhishna Pannikot

National Institute of Technology Karnataka

and

Tanupriya

CHRIST (Deemed to be University), Delhi NCR

The book presents a multi-faceted exploration of queer identities, narratives, and politics across literature, media, and popular culture. The collection engages with both Indian and global contexts, reflecting on how queer representation has evolved within these cultural landscapes. The book interrogates how different social, political, and historical frameworks shape the portrayal of queerness. This collection of essays critically analyzes queer sexualities through contemporary narratives, addressing gaps in existing scholarship. While queer studies in India is an emergent area, much of the academic focus has traditionally centered around women's representation, feminism, and masculinities. In contrast, scholarship specifically addressing queer sexualities and trans experiences through literature and media remains underrepresented. In India, legal advances such as the decriminalization of same-sex relationships have paved the way for a more public discourse on queerness, but these debates are still shaped by complex intersections of identity, culture, and power. This collection of essays seeks to fill this critical gap by examining queer subjectivities and representations through the frameworks of gender, identity, history, nationalism, and censorship.

At the same time, the book features chapters that engage with queer scholarship from other contexts, particularly the US. By including studies on US-based media and literary narratives, the book not only offers a comparative lens, but also reflects the transnational nature of queer experiences and scholarship. The focus on these two specific loci, India and the US, allows for a nuanced understanding of how cultural and political contexts shape the articulation and visibility of queer identities differently. The rationale behind this comparative framework lies in recognizing the distinct histories of LGBTQ+ movements in both countries, while also examining the shared challenges posed by heteronormativity, neoliberal politics, and media representation. This dual focus makes the volume relevant to both regional and global scholarship, offering insights into the complexities and convergences of queer representation across different cultural milieus.

The decision to foreground both Indian and American contexts is intentional, as it allows for a comparative exploration of how queerness is framed, resisted, or celebrated in different socio-political climates. While Indian narratives emphasize the vernacular complexities of gender and sexuality, US-based studies focus on issues such as queer migration, asexuality, and the politics of media representation. By bringing together these two loci, the book highlights the ways in which queer bodies and narratives resist dominant frameworks across multiple cultural spaces. However, recent years have witnessed a growing visibility of LGBTQAI+ issues, especially in light of the landmark events like the decriminalization of Section 377 and the rise of digital platforms as spaces for queer expression and activism. The current debates in India revolve around themes such as legal recognition of same-sex relationships; the inclusion of non-binary identities; queer representations in popular media; and the intersections of caste, religion, and gender. This book addresses these emerging conversations and critically explores the shifting narratives that portray queerness within Indian culture.

The book is divided into three parts: Part 1 – Queer Possibilities: Power Dynamics and Agency in Cinema and Literature, Part 2 – Embodying Intersectionality, and Part 3 – Vernacular Perspectives. Each section examines distinct domains of queer representation that challenge heteronormative frameworks and offer alternative imaginaries. The book aims to critically examine queer representations in twenty-first-century narratives, providing scope to understand and investigate these cultural representations that depict current debates and queer politics.

Part 1 of the book examines how queer identities navigate social spaces marked by vulnerability, nationalism, and systemic inequality. Chapters in this section explore narratives that reflect the intersection of queerness with religion, cultural stigma, and power dynamics. Part 2 focuses on the intersections of queerness with race, disability, and media representation. These chapters delve into complex identities, exploring topics like Black feminist epistemologies, asexuality, and trans identities. By addressing both dehumanization and hypersexualization in media, this section interrogates how queer and trans individuals are represented in global narratives. Part 3 centers on the cultural specificities of queer representation within localized frameworks, such as Assamese cinema and postcolonial literature. These chapters highlight how local stories and contexts frame queer identities, creating unique expressions of desire and resistance that are deeply rooted in vernacular cultures.

This literary work presents a significant contribution to queer scholarship, offering perspectives that are both locally grounded and globally relevant. The comprehensive array of themes examined within this volume will be invaluable for scholars and researchers interested in gender, sexuality, literature, and popular culture, providing a foundation for future research in these areas. By engaging with contemporary debates in India and beyond, this volume invites readers to critically reflect on the evolving politics of queer representation and its transformative potential in the twenty-first century.

Part 1 of the book, "Queer Possibilities: Power Dynamics and Agency in Cinema and Literature," includes four chapters.

Chapter 1 presents a detailed analysis of Shyam Selvadurai's *Funny Boy* (1994) and Nemat Sadat's *The Carpet Weaver* (2019). The chapter focuses on the development of social identity and behavioral patterns that affect sexuality. It provides insights on the impact of cultural metaphors on the male body from infancy by projecting queer identities in social spaces of vulnerability in the form of sexual abuse and violence perpetrated by the heteronormative society. It discusses complex ideas like compulsory heterosexism in the context of religion, vulnerability and social inequality, and stigma towards homosexuality.

Chapter 2, "(Im-)Mobile Sexualities and Queer Possibilities in *Angry Queer Somali Boy* (2019) by Mohamed Abdulkarim Ali," presents nationalism and mobility through the lens of sexuality and queer migration studies. This chapter provides insights into understanding a memoir based on transcultural existences in relation to local and global identities of nation-states that are reinforced and protected by state control mechanisms. The chapter focuses on the challenges faced by queer refugees in a heteropatriarchal system, emphasizing their presence and the need for discussion in global literature.

Chapter 3, "Unveiling the Embodied Nexus: Interrogating the Interplay of Queer and Crip Identities in the Cinematic Landscape of *Margarita with a Straw*," presents an in-depth analysis of the film's narrative, characters, and cinematic techniques to navigate the complexities of queerness and disability, challenging traditional notions of identity, sexuality, and bodily autonomy. Drawing upon queer theory and disability studies, this chapter investigates the nuanced representation of the protagonist in the film. This chapter closely examines the film's visual and auditory elements, uncovering how cinematography, sound design, and mise-en-scène contributes to the representation of queer and crip experiences. By analyzing the film's aesthetic choices, this research aims to reveal the cinematic techniques employed to challenge and subvert dominant narratives surrounding queerness and disability.

Chapter 4, "Shahria Sharmin's *Call Me Heena*: Decolonial Heterotopic Space of the Photograph and Representation of the Hijra," focuses on hijra communities who face extreme marginalization due to their exclusion from nearly all aspects of society. Although the hijras have captured the interests (and imagination) of photographers since early colonial photography, a limited number of projects, like Dhaka-based freelance photographer Shahria Sharmin's *Call Me Heena* (2012-2014), attempt to portray the hijra subjectivity. Through this chapter, it is emphasized that the intimate portraits are an attempt to decolonize the hijras, as these images show a shift from the ethnographic (colonial) eye to a focus on their subjectivity. The photographic space serves as a counter-space that differs from both mainstream society and the sites regularly inhabited by hijras. This chapter focuses on photographing the hijras' journey from Bangladesh to India. Through the simple, dark background reminiscent of a studio, the character de-emphasizes the external elements and dislocates the hijra from the colonial structure of the photograph and reality, instead, creating room for their social structures, practices, and desires to shine.

Part 2 of this book, "Embodying Intersectionality," includes three chapters. Chapter 5, "Liberated from the Binary: An Interrogation of Gender in Rivers Solomon's *An Unkindness of Ghosts* and *The Deep*", focuses on Black feminist epistemologies in *An Unkindness of Ghosts* (2017) and *The Deep* (2019) that expand notions of racial and gender-based identities. "Ungendering" as a key concept by Spiller is examined in this chapter to present intersectional struggles and project how gender is used by social structures as a mode of restraint. The chapter further focuses on how fracture creates ways to liberate the world through Black feminist embodied knowledge.

Chapter 6, "Trans and Asexual Representation: Between Oversexualization and Dehumanization," offers a brief timeline of LGBT+ representation in US media, with a focus on television and the transition to streaming. Asexual and trans representation share an interesting parallel: Asexual individuals are often depicted as inhuman due to their lack of sexual interest, while trans individuals are frequently over-sexualized and portrayed in a predatory manner. Some of the most positive representations are now emerging in children's television, mirroring the recent surge of strong LGBT+ representation in young adult literature.

Chapter 7, "The Monstrous Rainbow Swastika: The Horror Genre's Queer Nazi versus Historical Fact," explores how the lack of understanding surrounding queer persecution during the Holocaust has led to two significant outcomes. First, Hollywood, particularly in sensational genres like horror, has exploited Nazism to portray queer characters as more frightening and predatory. Second, this has resulted in the rise of the mythical 'queer Nazi' in popular culture, a trope that not only distorts history but also further alienates audiences from the realities of the Holocaust.

Part 3 of this book, "Vernacular Perspectives," includes one chapter. Chapter 8, "Macho Girl to Poster Girl: Precarious Lives and the Heteronormative Social Order in Himanjali Sankar's *Talking of Muskaan* (2014)" explores Muskaan's predicament through the lens of 'precarity.' The paper will attempt to complicate the social processes of 'girling' and, consequently, defamiliarize the safety of the classroom by upholding it as an allegory for the precarious postcolonial nation-state through the trajectory of Muskaan's lived experiences as an outed lesbian.

This volume brings together diverse perspectives from authors around the world, offering critical insights into queer representations and their intersections with popular culture. The editors acknowledge and appreciate the contributors for engaging with a wide range of themes, contexts, and methodologies, and for presenting stimulating arguments that explore various dimensions of queer representations in literature and popular culture.

PART 1:
QUEER POSSIBILITIES:
POWER DYNAMICS AND
AGENCY IN CINEMA AND
LITERATURE

Chapter One
Discipline or Abuse: Policing the Gender Narratives of Queer Identities and Body Image Through *Funny Boy* and *The Carpet Weaver*

Sanjana Chakraborty
National Institute of Technology Sikkim, India
and
Dhananjay Tripathi
National Institute of Technology Sikkim, India

Abstract

Despite extensive research across various domains such as psychology, medicine, and culture on queer identities in South Asia, a persistent gap remains in examining the influence of patriarchal masculinity and heteronormative ideologies on queer bodies. Several cases of sexual assault like Hamed Sabouri's execution by the Taliban in Afghanistan (*The Guardian* 2022) and Sri Lanka's forced anal exams on queer individuals since 2017 (*Human Rights Watch* 2020) are overlooked in the mainstream discussions of gender-based violence. Thus, the chapter focuses on the need to examine gender identity and body fluidity, which are often restrained within the bounds of religion and culture in South Asian discourse. Moreover, it analyzes the socio-political forces or biopolitical forces that shape the configuration of gender narratives, influencing the construction of identity and sexuality. Through Shyam Selvadurai's *Funny Boy* (1994) and Nemat Sadat's *The Carpet Weaver* (2019), the chapter illustrates how cultural metaphors and political unrest influence the male body from infancy, creating spaces of inequality. Arjie and Kanishka, the protagonists, embody the scars of societal ideals that subject queer male bodies to violence and sexual abuse. It highlights how heteronormative privilege creates vulnerabilities within queer identities, forcing them into compulsory heterosexuality, driven by cultural and religious markers, resulting in compounded marginalization and inequality.

Moreover, migrating across national borders introduces uncertainty and change in cultural definitions of sexuality for non/normative identities. It escalates through homophobic stigma as the construction of identities is culturally formulated. Thus, the chapter identifies these patterns in which one's body is socially constructed and regulated, adhering to the geo-political specifics and marginalizing their gendered experiences within public and private spaces.

Keywords: Queer Identities, Social Policies of Gender, Queer Body Image, Identity Politics.

***

Introduction

The inception of masculinity studies was to contest the linear view of masculinity, which is performed in alignment with appropriate male mannerisms. Thus, questioning the oversimplification of male identity in contrast to female identity compromises its intricate construction. Meanwhile, Rutherford formulates "New Man" and the "Retributive Man" (Rutherford 1998, 28 cited in Hobbs 2013, 384) as the metaphoric portrayal of masculinity. This relates to the repressed social descriptions of masculinity and how the male bodies are consistently shaped by bio-markers aligned with social norms.

These definitions further accentuate the meaning of hegemonic masculinity, which are practices of "socially accepted masculine behaviours and beliefs within a given time and culture" (Bauermeister et al. 2016, 1). As a result, it creates the space of inequalities for men of sexual minorities and their psychological well-being, while these reckonable associations remain an uncharted arena. The chapter, consequently, focuses on understanding everyday negotiations of masculine identifications, which are mostly biopolitical, by the young queer bodies within the South Asian contexts.

The Carpet Weaver (2019) by Nemat Sadat portrays Kanishka Nurzada's journey toward self-acceptance as a young gay boy in Afghanistan, a society that is defined by oppressive religious ideologies and homophobic views on masculine norms. Set during the Saur Revolution (1978), it encircles three locations: life in Afghanistan, exile in Pakistan, and migration to America. It mirrors the internal and external struggle of Kanishka that navigates the cultural repression and identity negotiations across borders. Narrated from Kanishka's perspective, it reflects his experiences of being gay and the complexities of forced displacement and identity formation. Moreover, his relations with Maihan and Faiz showcase the dangers of being gay or *kuni-ha* (a derogatory term for gay in Afghanistan), where homosexuality is criminalized, and survival involves resisting brutality and societal persecution.

Shyam Selvadurai's *Funny Boy* (1994), divided into six stories, presents Arjie's bildungsroman narrative against the backdrop of the Tamil-Sinhalese Civil War of 1983. Tracing back seven years of his childhood before the riots and adolescence, and his family's subsequent migration to Canada, the novel builds within the memories of a lost homeland in Sri Lanka. It particularly focuses on his journey of self-discovery as a sexual minority, especially in the chapters *Pigs Can't Fly* and *Best School of All*, where Arjie's emerging sexuality clashes with his family's rigid ideals of masculinity in a country where homosexuality is illegal.

South Asian heterosexism, rooted in culture and religion, poses significant challenges for queer boys as portrayed in these narratives. Their sexualities confront the hegemonic masculine identity and therefore are not granted the "biopolitical privilege" (Bunds 2014, 514-515) with which heterosexual males, at least, are accorded. This privilege is attached to "sex role identity" (Reeser 2015, 96) and maintained psychosocially through masculine or feminine gestures. The chapter illustrates how identity politics further marginalizes queer bodies. Socio-political activity influences discrimination based on "group members because of differences or conflicts between their particular identity" (Duignan 2023, 1). Socially inscribed masculinity becomes invisible within heteronormative frameworks, thus acting as a promulgator of patriarchal power. These intricacies, which intersect between gender, sex, and desire, can most powerfully reveal the limitations of stereotypical male roles, particularly when the study of masculinity intersects with queer theory.

Mapping Methodology Through Theoretical Interventions

This chapter adopts a qualitative methodology and is grounded in textual analysis, drawing primarily on theoretical frameworks from Butler's performativity, Reeser's understanding of masculinity, Foucault's biopolitics, and Crenshaw's intersectionality. Such perspectives are synthesized with the postcolonial approaches of scholars like Gayatri Gopinath and Spivak, among others. It aims to address the specific issues that queer individuals in South Asia face due to the criminalization of homosexuality in certain regions of the area. Recent queer identities scholarship describes how the intersecting elements of social politics, class, ethnicity, and religion are shaping LGBTQIA+ lives within South Asian discourse.

Contributions from scholars like Kareem Khubchandani with their analysis of queer nightlife in India in their work *Ishtyle (2020)*, Rangnekar's analysis of being queer in India and Thailand in his work *QueerSapien (2023)*, and Jasbir Puar illustrate how queer bodies are policed and struggle economically and socially. This chapter situates the experiences of Arjie (*Funny Boy*) and Kanishka (*The Carpet Weaver*) to confirm that marginalization is deeply rooted within heteronormative cultural and religious norms in Sri Lanka and Afghanistan. Gopinath studies queer diaspora through the prism of the global spectrum of queer persecution. Thus, the novels act as evidence of social criticism toward these coercive social norms which promote queer violence.

Both novels highlight the resulting spaces of inequality created by cultural metaphors that regulate male bodies from infancy onward. South Asian cultural and religious paradigms glorify heterosexism in a way that produces homophobia, both legally and morally, in Afghanistan and Sri Lanka. This fuels the use of sodomy, more evasively termed "corrective rape" (Chakraborty and Tripathi 2023, 83), as a tool to regulate queer bodies. In doing so, it reveals the systematic oppression and exclusion of queer boys like Arjie and Kanishka by blending normative masculinity with identity politics. The text further scrutinizes the violence imposed on queer male bodies based on these ideologies. The chapter explores how the social positioning of patriarchal men exacerbates the vulnerabilities and exclusion of LGBTQIA+ communities, making them more susceptible to abuse. This will be interpreted through the lenses of men's studies, queer theory, and postcolonialism.

Changing Dynamics of Masculinity and Male Body Image Issue

"My skin is a map. A map of my world. My secret world. It tells you where I've been. And how to get to where I come from" (Miller, 1994, 321 cited in Berry 2007, 263).

The definitions of manhood have undergone a historical shift in certain parts of the world, moving toward more inclusive and less restrictive norms of 'manhood.' However, boys consecutively experience societal pressure to follow the mannerisms of the dominant forms of masculinity through gender policing. The cultural morphology of various forms of masculine ideals, such as the dandy, metrosexual, marketplace man, etc., coincided with these shifting dynamics.

It is within the culture that sexuality becomes a key site of contestation, racialization, and ideological power. Furthermore, the migration adds to the marginalized identity, where the traditional South Asian cultures clash with Western white masculinity. Jasbir Puar (2007) introduces the concept of "homonationalism," building on ideas of homonormativity to demonstrate how gay rights can be intertwined with neo-imperial nation-building projects and foreign interventions. In *Manhood in America* (1996), Micheal Kimmel defined the two key elements of writing about men as men: "first, to chart how the definition of masculinity has changed over time; second, to explore how the experience of manhood has shaped the activities of American men" (Reeser 2015, 19). A similar analogy is examined in the context of masculinity within the South Asian discourse, which is shaped by religious and socio-political circumstances as depicted in the novels. The terror of civil war implicitly affects the queer bodies as they carry the scars of abuse and trauma in the physical and psychological spectrum within the public and private spheres.

The chapter elaborates on these experiences of young gay male bodies within the South Asian discourse through Crenshaw's Intersectional approach. Kimberlé Crenshaw coined the term *Intersectionality* in her article *Demarginalizing the Intersection of Race and Sex* (1989). It was published in the University of Chicago Legal Forum to highlight the unique experience of discrimination faced by Black women. In one of her recent interviews with *Time* (2020), she stated, "Intersectionality is a lens through which you can see where power comes and collides, where it interlocks and intersects" (Katy 2020). However, the chapter incorporates Gayatri Spivak Chakraborty's postcolonial concept of the 'subaltern,' as this intersection of sexuality and power challenges the traditional marginalization of voices like Arjie and Kanishka in both novels. The chapter utilizes Spivak's lens to explore how colonial legacies shape queer identities as 'other,' further marginalizing LGBTQIA+ individuals within the postcolonial nation. Kanishka in *The Carpet Weaver* (2019) is constantly torn between his acceptance of his sexuality and social reality: "I felt trapped, wondering whether I should choose a life pleasing Maihan and my heart's desire or serving Baba and the revolution. It would be impossible to have one without losing the other" (Sadat 2019, 127). Thus, both Arjie in *Funny Boy* (1994) and Kanishka in *The Carpet Weaver* (2019) symbolize the "subaltern in terms of race, sexuality or gender" (Rao 1997, 118).

Integrating these notions, this chapter explores the unique challenges faced by South Asian homosexual boys, which are further intensified in conflict or war zones, deepening their sense of alienation. Given the nature of gender dynamics, it is crucial to observe that male bodies, especially those with non-conforming sexualities, such as Arjie and Kanishka, experience significant societal pressure within their domestic spaces. Moreover, the world outside abides by the culturally designed heterosexist male behavior to legitimize their male bodies and marginalize queer identities.

Performative Inscriptions on the Male Body

In *The Carpet Weaver* (2019), Kanishka celebrates his sixteenth birthday in Kabul, marking the beginning of his youth. His godfather, Zaki Jaan, remarks, "The one thing I know is that Allah never forgives sodomy" (Sadat 2019, 3, cited in Chakraborty and Tripathi 2023, 76), establishing the underlying conflict between religious doctrine and sexual identity. Kanishka and Maihan are destined to walk different paths—Kanishka pursues sexual freedom in America, carrying the scars left by Pakistan's camp leader, Tor Gul, while Maihan remains trapped under the weight of familial expectations and rigid cultural ideals of masculinity. Maihan's character is the embodiment of the internal strife between his self-perception and the demands of "patriarchal masculinity" (Chakraborty and Tripathi 2023, 80) that is rooted in his society's Islamic construct. Furthermore, Maihan and Kanishka face the trauma of life threats and school harassment in Kabul, where Maihan expresses his fear, "I received a letter from an unknown source... saying ... they will gang rape us, take our photos and expose us as Kuni-Ha to everyone" (Sadat 2019, 113, cited in Chakraborty and Tripathi 2023, 82). Unfamiliar with such atrocities and trauma faced within these spaces of social institutions, Maihan lived under constant "fear of being identified as kuni-ha" (Chakraborty and Tripathi 2023, 82).

After the migration to America, Maihan chooses to keep his sexuality closeted and solidifies this through the bonds of marriage with his cousin Lamba to conform to the cultural narratives of his homeland. He views this marital bond as conforming to his status as a man, stating, "I'm becoming a real man" (Sadat 2019, 271 cited in Chakraborty and Tripathi 2023, 85). The traditionalist association of *biopolitical privilege* is linked with the hegemonic male body. However, Maihan and Kanishka lose their "male privilege" (Chakraborty and Tripathi 2023, 77) and biopolitical standing, as they resist hegemonic masculinity, a reality starkly explored through these textual references in the novel.

Similarly, in *Funny Boy (1994)*, Arjie realizes his differing masculinity when he is humiliated in front of his family in the drawing room of his house, which is a semi-public space, by his Kanthi Aunty for playing, *bride-bride*, along with his female cousins adorned in a saree, in the chapter *Pigs Can't Fly*,

> "She dragged me through the kitchen,...and towards the drawing room...Instinctively, I knew that Kanthi Aunty had something terrible in mind. As we entered the drawing room...her voice brimming over with laughter, see what I found!" (Selvadurai 1994, 13).

Seeing his appearance, Arjie's uncle calls him the "Funny One" (Selvadurai 1994, 13), addressing his father, whose silent stares give the obvious impression of disagreement and the family's perception towards differing masculinity as humorous. This leads to a heated argument between his parents, where the mother is blamed for his behavior, as she allows him to watch her getting dressed for occasions. The next day, his mother forces him to play cricket, asserting, "You're a big boy now. And big boys must play with other boys"

(Selvadurai 1994, 20). Since cricket is associated with masculine imagery and other biopolitical metaphors, such as economic and social standing through Chelva's (Arjie's father) hotelier business, it reflects the social positioning of Tamil male identity. Thus, the childhood act of innocence attached to these biopolitical metaphors highlights the enforced norm of masculine conformity in a rigid, war-torn environment.

There is a similar incident of confrontation in *The Carpet Weaver (2019)*, between Kanishka's mother (Maadar) and Maihan's mother, where the latter comes to the former's home to confront her about a love letter sent by Kanishka to Maihan, after Kanishka's father's demise. Maihan's mother directly asserts to Maadar, "Don't you know? Kanishka has been pursuing my Maihan. Maadar protested… 'They're just friends'" (Sadat 2019, 162). Maihan's mother refutes this assertion and states, "I thought only those dirty old men from Kandahar, Kunar, and Kunduz preyed on boys. I never imagined a Kabuli boy would be a kuni!" (Sadat 2019, 162). After this episode, Kanishka feels humiliated because his secret had been revealed in an inappropriate way. He knows his mother didn't hate him for his reality but did not "accept me for who I truly was" (Sadat, 2019, 163). The parallel between these two scenes from two distinct novels set in separate geographical countries emphasizes how difficult it is for queer identities to survive in a world where orthodox gender narratives transcend national borders.

These instances illustrate the concept of gender performativity, as proposed by Judith Butler in *Gender Trouble*. Butler states, "…tenuously constituted in time, instituted in an exterior space through *a stylized repetition of acts*" (Butler 2002, 179). Furthermore, these acts accentuate the biopolitical control, where bodies are regulated and policed through social institutions. In Afghanistan and Sri Lanka, social identities are shaped by strict cultural norms reinforced by religious beliefs. The use of "strategic essentialism" (Spivak 1996, 214 cited in Höpflinger et al. 2012, 615-638) is implied when identity politics are based on religion and idealized gender relationships.

This intersectional approach, coupled with Spivak's "strategic essentialism" (Spivak 1996, 214 cited in Höpflinger et al. 2012, 615-638) shows how Western and South Asian literary works analyze the distinctive strain of being a South Asian homosexual. In D. H. Lawrence's *Women in Love* (1920), the gladiatorial wrestling scene between Gerald and Birkin serves as a moment of emotional attunement, nurturing connection through physical intimacy. Similarly, in *The Carpet Weaver*, this dynamic is mirrored in the attraction between Kanishka and Maihan, who are drawn to each other but restrained by religious obligations in a comparable wrestling setting. In this respect, Arjie's journey in *Funny Boy* corresponds to Edmund White's *Boys Own Room* (1982), but, the layered identity in Arjie brings together the sexual, ethnic, and displaced dimensions within South Asian paradigms, which "all speak of multiple displacements and exiles" (Gopinath 2005, 144). Still, unlike the Western context where homosexuality is a privileged space, as Gayatri Gopinath points out, he is in a "singular site of radical difference and the narrator's sole claim to alterity" (Gopinath 2003, 144). This chapter thus maps the distinct negotiation of homosexuality in South Asian male bodies, differing from Western experiences.

Impact on Policy Making and Social Mediascape

The cultural demarcation of South Asian family structures adorned with the paradigms of traditionalism forces the non-heteronormative kids to remain concealed within the closet. The cultural inscriptions on the male body are subjected to these variable social factors. This creates an alienating space where the 'differing' masculinity is equated with a "hysterical female body" (Reeser 2010, 96) constructed within the social discourse of gender dynamics. The strife left behind by the footprints of draconian colonial laws is very much alive in the present-day legal frameworks of Sri Lanka. For example, Section 365A criminalizes homosexuality, which escalates queer marginalization. Human rights activists, like Ambika Satkunanathan, identify this residue of colonial legacies as feeding into modern jurisprudence by claiming deviant masculinity *against the order of nature*. Besides, after *Funny Boy* (1994) was read by the then President of Sri Lanka, he considered "repealing anti-sodomy laws" (Salgado 2004, 7), which activated a nationwide debate. Eventually, a landmark shift was reported in May 2023 by CNN, where the Sri Lankan Supreme Court considered "clearing the path to decriminalizing homosexuality" (Reuters 2023).

Likewise, in Afghanistan, uncodified Sharia law prohibits same-sex acts among men and women, with maximum sentencing of the death penalty. Particularly for such acts, Article 130's provisions, such as Section 646 (Sodomy) and Section 645 (Musahaqah), specify severe punishments. After the 2021 Taliban reacquisition and reestablishment of the Islamic Emirate, these laws have become more stringent.

However, the practice of *bacha baazi* (often associated with certain military factions, where young boys are abducted for the sexual exploitation of adult men) persists. In this context, same-sex acts or sodomy are often used as symbols of male dominance and power, rather than being linked to LGBTQIA+ identities. The widespread misconception that equates homosexuality with prostitution or deviance continues to heavily influence the legal framework in this country. A 2007 report showed that laws for restricting *bacha baazi* were presented; however, the execution seems to be a far-fetched dream to be achieved in a country ruled by arms and weapons.

Various outlets, like Human Rights Watch and OutRight Action International (2022), have recently reported on how Afghans live in fear as a result of the Taliban's resurgence, as well as its situation with the country's LGBTQIA+ community. First-hand accounts describe rampant violence and kidnappings, mob attacks, and gang rapes. The current situation in Taliban-ruled Afghanistan highlights, through these reports, how social media platforms serve as traps to track down queer individuals, monitoring and policing them to conform to normative cultures. NGOs like *Roshaniya*, a US-based organization with which the Nemat Sadat is associated, help provide psychosocial support and long-term resettlement options. Sadat has been upfront through his social media presence on Instagram and Twitter about supporting these operations and protesting against this gender apartheid.

Thus, the chapter focuses on these narratives to demonstrate the need for grassroots activism within the state and the patriarchal gaze of families. It also emphasizes the importance of adopting an intersectional approach to understanding queer identities. Moreover, these pieces of evidence will help policymakers, educators, and activists to reduce stigma, promote inclusivity, and focus on changing the narrative towards intersectional oppression.

Policing or Abuse: Effects of Gender Narratives and Queer Identities

The cultural narratives encircling gender understanding often create spaces of abuse, both physical and emotional, for those who acknowledge their queer subjectivity. In 2018, the *Harvard Business Review* observed that men who are inclined towards feminine traits often face the brunt of social criticism. That is similar to women who are inclined towards masculine traits. Thus, gender policing incorporates the coercion of heteronormative gender expressions employing the weapon of abuse under the guise of discipline by the patriarchal heterosexist figures.

However, studies have underscored that "Gender policing during childhood and adolescence was associated with recent substance use behaviors and psychological distress in multivariable models" (Bauermeister et al. 2016, 1). Moreover, negative reinforcement is typically employed to discourage nonconformity in children. In Sadat's *The Carpet Weaver* (2019) and Selvadurai's *Funny Boy* (1994), the voices of marginalized male bodies are framed within traditional masculine standards. Both novels depict the negative reinforcements faced by Arjie and Kanishka, the protagonists, who experience threats from their families and the guilt imposed upon them. In *Men of the World (2015)*, Jeff Hearn identifies the significance of acknowledging "men and masculinities as explicitly gendered" (Allan 2020, 72) in correlation to the "gendered power" (Allan 2020, 72) of social power dynamics. Families and educational institutes act as gendered spaces, playing a crucial role in policing non/normative identities, often demoralizing feminine mannerisms in sons, "encouraging the male child to police his gender expression and/or behavior" (Hill and Menviele 2009, 243-71 cited in Bauermeister et al. 2016, 2). Studies underscore that non/normative male children who are coerced into masculine behaviors are prone to "use alcohol, marijuana or substance abuse" and showcase varied levels of "depressive and anxiety symptoms" (Bauermeister et al. 2016, 6).

These symptoms of psychological distress are augmented by the pervasive policing of queer identities' gender performance by the families. Another familiar space for gender policing is schools, as described in the novels, where the act of sodomy is used like a weapon to "correct the wrong" (Chakraborty and Tripathi 2023, 83). This explores the negotiation of biopolitical spaces wherein bodies, as the medium of regulation and control, are used in the reinforcement of hegemonic values by social powers. Foucault describes this phenomenon, "biopolitics," as "the processes by which human life, at the population level, emerged as a distinct political problem in Western societies" (Means 2018, 1).

As observed in the textual evidence of the narratives, while at their academic institution, Maihan and Kanishka (The Carpet Weaver) go to a secluded space to discuss Maihan's venture into being a CIA agent. They discuss the effects of the Saur Revolution and their future in the West for a better life, when their classmates come and yank open the door and pull them out:

> "They took us by the collar, by the throat …We were in real danger now. They hauled us out and spun us around like spindles, each rotation accompanied by punches … each boy grabbing and violating a different part of our bodies . . . This was a circus, and Maihan and I the entertainment" (Sadat 2019, 148).

The assault scene serves to heighten the power of toxic masculinity and homophobia, in which sodomy or corrective rape forms punishment to 'correct' what religion and law condemn. These assaults by their classmates were methods employed to make Kanishka and Maihan prove their manhood. This episode of systematic violence against male bodies highlights the acts of sexual harassment often silenced in popular culture. This further eliminates the space for queer male identities to be seen as victims, instead deepening their marginalization.

Similarly, in *Funny Boy* (1994), Arjie's transfer to Queen Victoria Academy is to impose traditional manhood; his father, Chelva, declares, "The Academy will force you to become a man" (Selvadurai 1994, 210). His brother Diggy cautions him that, once admitted, boys are expected to transition into manhood, saying,

"Either you take it like a man, or the other boys will look down upon you" (Selvadurai 1994, 211). Through Sri Lanka's British-influenced private schooling, this gendered social agenda of creating colonized men is emphasized in these narratives. These further integrate Foucault's *concept of surveillance*, weaved into the Panopticon social structure, where Arjie is constantly monitored for sexual deviations. This surveillance moves beyond his domestic boundaries to national repression, accentuating the intricacies of the biopolitical landscape. Influenced by colonial legacies and homophobic views around homosexuality, the Sri Lankan state exercises control over the bodies of sexual minorities within the social dynamic. Diggy's interpretation of the Head Prefect and Shehan's relationship and assault on a Tamil Boy in Queen Victoria Academy are examples of nationalist conflicts infiltrating educational institutes, promoting violence-imbued dominance.

> "I say Cheliah, Salgado said, don't you know better than to come to the toilet unaccompanied...Salgado gave a signal and the boys grabbed Cheliah ... one of the boys swiftly put his hand over Cheliah's mouth, silencing his cries..." (Selvadurai 1994, 219).

This kind of forced sexual behavior is consistently practiced within the school premises and the authorities turn a blind eye to it; rather, they use it as a weapon to prevent queer identities from being revealed and to build up fear-induced heterosexism. These kinds of behavior also encourage communal riots between Sinhalese and Tamilians and prove the social power held over one another. His brother Diggy and others enjoy this *biopolitical privilege*, but Arjie, being the queer boy, loses this privilege living under constant threat and suffering psychologically. Arjie's realization of non-acceptance of his sexuality came from his father's displeasure with naming his reality as "...certain tendencies " (Selvadurai 1994, 166) while convincing Jegan to make Arjie more manly. His father's allusion to his diverse sexuality as a tendency grounds Arjie's loss of *biopolitical privilege* without ever giving it a name.

Both narratives act as representations of an adolescent gay boy living in Afghanistan and Sri Lanka, where homosexuality is legally prohibited. Kanishka (protagonist of *The Carpet Weaver)* and Arjie (protagonist of *Funny Boy)* endure the pain of exclusion and mental trauma born out of the traditional gender policing that socio-political and religious structures impose on queer male bodies. Another striking element in both stories is that they use home and school environments to show how the politics of the land affect individual gender stories during periods of national and ethnic conflict. For Kanishka and Arjie, their cultural background is central to their identities, as the politics of their specific locality influence how men are perceived within their families.

Contemporary Social and Personal Impact of Gender Policing

Years after the publication of *Funny Boy* (1994) and its transformation into a major motion picture, gender policing issues remain evident in Sri Lanka. A recent report by Human Rights Watch (HRW) and EQUAL GROUND (2020) states that "Sri Lankan authorities have subjected at least seven people to forced physical examinations since 2017" (HRW 2020), striving to collect proof of possible homosexual conduct. These procedures, which include forced anal and vaginal exams, are associated with sexual abuse and constitute inhumane treatment that can escalate to torture. As a result, the fear of such horrors causes queer individuals to become increasingly closeted.

Since the Taliban's return to power in Afghanistan in 2021, the LGBTQIA+ community has faced severe persecution, living in constant fear of violence due to their sexual orientation. Nemat Sadat recently noted that the novel "acts as a mirror of present Afghanistan while giving the image of the past" (Chakraborty and Tripathi 2023, 87). As per reports published by *The Guardian* on October 18, 2022, a young man named Hamed Sabouri was executed for the alleged crime of being a homosexual, and the execution video was sent to his family. After the takeover staged by Taliban fighters, numerous gay men have been detained, beaten, and sexually abused.

Since the reacquisition, human rights activists like Sima Samar (now in exile) started a campaign in 2023 for *gender apartheid*, the systematic oppression of women and diverse genders, which is a crime against humanity to be recognized under UN international law. However, these voices have been completely unheard, and as Mairiam Safi, an activist, states, "It is becoming easy for policymakers and international decision-makers to ignore Afghan women in exile" (Kelly 2024). Nemat Sadat, in a recent interview with *Kabul Now*, points out the dire situation of Afghan queer communities and how they have "no future in Afghanistan under Taliban rule…they risk getting tortured to death" (Iltaf 2024, 2). In January 2024, a study was conducted with 3,600 women, of whom 67% agreed that the restrictions they lived under contribute to a systematic oppression. Similarly, in a 48-page report conducted by OutRight Action International (2022) where 60 Afghan queer individuals were interviewed, many stated the plight they face at the hands of the Taliban. A gay man said that Taliban members detained him at a checkpoint, beat him, and gang-raped him, telling him, "… we will do whatever we want with you." (HRW 2022). A Taliban spokesperson told *Reuters* (2021) in October, "LGBT … That's against our Sharia [Islamic] law." Despite making repeated pledges to respect human rights, marked by systematic abuse of power combined with vitriolic anti-LGBTQIA+ sentiment, Taliban officials and their supporters have carried out acts of violence against LGBTQIA+ people.

Thus, the chapter utilizes these reports to focus on the plight of queer individuals in real-time social scenarios. The constant surveillance of national borders and financial instability limit resettlement options, while the fear of queer persecution contributes to the deterioration of mental health and the denial of basic human rights for queer individuals.

Conclusion

The present research indicates a clear link between psychological distress and gender policing, with those aware of such pressures experiencing heightened anxiety and despair. Hegemonic masculinity is associated with its traditional male attributes—domination, aggression, violence, and strength. It operates within a complex interplay of social forces that extends beyond the "contest of brute power into the organization, private life, and cultural process" (Yalley et al. 2020, 1). This complex performance of masculinity frequently excludes sexual minority men, reinforcing social norms that label their identities as aberrant. The chapter's analysis of the queer narratives in *Funny Boy* (1994) and *The Carpet Weaver* (2019) demonstrates that the systemic marginalization of queer identities across South Asia continues, rooted in colonial legacies and religious control. This intervenes with the efforts of inclusivity and aids the heteronormative ideals to create spaces of queer marginalization.

It highlights the intersectional nature of South Asian queer experiences that are shaped by the socio-political factors and issues of class, ethnicity, and religion that embody sexual identities. It investigates the efficacy of community-led interventions and digital platforms in forming queer identity. It focuses on the imposition of colonial residues in queer narratives that impact the country's legal frameworks and, in turn, affect queer identities. Thus, decolonizing this requires dismantling these laws and challenging their residual impact on queer bodies. This is observed in the chapter through the use of the postcolonial lens of Gopinath and Spivak, who recognize how colonial histories still fuel the present-day struggles of queer identities.

However, this chapter has some limitations; therefore, future research could explore the particularities of queer migration studies and the unfolding global literary queer representations. Beyond that, legal system reforms must be implemented to ensure adequate protection for LGBTQIA+ people. Advocacy campaigns must work toward dismantling adverse popular cultural discourses and pertinent public education campaigns through art and architecture. It should serve as a part of promoting the representation of queer voices and valuing them as part of the sociocultural heritage in South Asia.

In summary, the chapter argues how the performative gender narrative turns young queer bodies into targets of violence while capturing such acts within a disciplinary framework. This is even more accentuated by the biopolitical theatres of family, schools, and militaries where soft control over the normalizing and pathologizing of deviant queer bodies is more dramatic. Therefore, the chapter concludes with a probing question: Are these acts of gender policing simply forms of discipline, or should they be recognized as abuse under international human rights law?

References

Allan, Jonathan A. "Queer Theory and Critical Masculinity Studies." In *Routledge International Handbook of Masculinity Studies*, 72–81. Routledge, 2019.

Bauermeister, José A., Daniel Connochie, Laura Jadwin-Cakmak, and Steven Meanley. "Gender Policing During Childhood and the Psychological Well-Being of Young Adult Sexual Minority Men in the United States." *American Journal of Men's Health* 11, no. 3 (2016): 693–701. https://doi.org/10.117 7/1557988316680938

Berry, Keith. "Embracing the Catastrophe: Gay Body Seeks Acceptance." *Qualitative Inquiry* 13, no. 2 (2007): 259–281. https://doi.org/10.1134/S00 81543807040177

Butler, Judith. *Gender Trouble: Feminism and the Subversion of Identity.* Routledge, 2002. https://doi.org/10.4324/9780203902752

Bunds, Kyle S. "The biopolitics of privilege: Negotiating class, masculinity, and relationships." Cultural Studies? Critical Methodologies 14, no. 5 (2014): 517-525. https://doi.org/10.1177/1532708614541895

Chakraborty, Sanjana, and Dhananjay Tripathi. "Influenced Gender Identities: The Study of Masculinity and Its Intersectionality through *The Carpet Weaver.*" *Boyhood Studies* 16, no. 1 (2023): 75–89.

Duignan, Brian. "Identity Politics." *Encyclopedia Britannica*, August 24, 2023. https://www.britannica.com/topic/identity-politics.

Gopinath, Gayatri. "Nostalgia, desire, diaspora: South Asian sexualities in motion." In Uprootings/Regroundings, pp. 137-156. Routledge, 2003.

Hassan, Hala. "Even If You Go to the Skies, We'll Find You: LGBT People in Afghanistan After the Taliban Takeover." *OutRight Action International*, January 26, 2022.

Hobbs, Alex. "Masculinity Studies and Literature." *Literature Compass* 10, no. 4 (2013): 383–395. https://doi.org/10.1111/lic3.12057

Höpflinger, Anna-Katharina, Anne Lavanchy, and Janine Dahinden. "Introduction: Linking Gender and Religion." *Women's Studies* 41, no. 6 (2012): 615–638. https://doi.org/10.1080/00497878.2012.691401.

Human Rights Watch. "Sri Lanka: Forced Anal Exams in Homosexuality Prosecutions." October 20, 2020. https://www.hrw.org/news/2020/10/20/ sri-lanka-forced-anal-exams-homosexuality-prosecutions.

Iltaf, Maissam. "Life for Afghanistan's LGBTs Was Already Hard, Then the Taliban Came." *Kabul Now*, February 7, 2024.

Kelly, Annie. "Afghan Women Fight to Hold Taliban to Account over Gender Apartheid." *The Guardian*, October 9, 2024.

Kimmel, Michael S. "The Contemporary 'Crisis' of Masculinity in Historical Perspective." In *The Making of Masculinities* (Routledge Revivals), 121–153. Routledge, 2018.

Rao, R. Raj. "Because Most People Marry Their Own Kind: A Reading of Shyam Selvadurai's *Funny Boy.*" *ARIEL: A Review of International English Literature* 28, no. 1 (1997): 117–128.

Reeser, Todd W. *Masculinities in Theory: An Introduction.* John Wiley & Sons, 2015.

Reuters. "Sri Lanka Supreme Court Clears Path to Decriminalize Homosexuality." *CNN News Blog,* May 9, 2023. https://edition.cnn.com/2023/05/09/asia/sri-lanka-decriminalize-homosexuality-supreme-court-intl-hnk/index.html.

Sadat, Nemat. *The Carpet Weaver.* Penguin Random House India Private Limited, 2019.

Salgado, Minoli. "Writing Sri Lanka, Reading Resistance: Shyam Selvadurai's *Funny Boy* and A. Sivanandan's *When Memory Dies.*" *The Journal of Commonwealth Literature* 39, no. 1 (2004): 5–18. https://doi.org/10.1177/002198904043283

Selvadurai, Shyam. *Funny Boy.* Penguin Random House India Private Limited, 1994.

Steinmetz, Katy. "She Coined the Term 'Intersectionality' Over 30 Years Ago. Here's What It Means to Her Today." *Time,* February 20, 2020.

Trust, Human Dignity. "Afghanistan." September 12, 2024. https://www.humandignitytrust.org/country-profile/afghanistan/.

Yalley, Abena Asefuaba, and Molatokunbo Seunfunmi Olutayo. "Gender, Masculinity and Policing: An Analysis of the Implications of Police Masculinized Culture on Policing Domestic Violence in Southern Ghana and Lagos, Nigeria." *Social Sciences & Humanities Open* 2, no. 1 (2020): 100077. https://doi.org/10.1016/j.ssaho.2020.100077

Chapter Two

(Im-) Mobile Sexualities and Queer Possibilities in *Angry Queer Somali Boy* (2019) by Mohamed Abdulkarim Ali

Ayse Irem Karabag
York University, Toronto

Abstract

In this chapter, as sexuality becomes the analytical lens by which I approach nationalism and mobility, I make an attempt at further exploration of what Eithne Luibhéid (2008) calls the "unruly body of inquiry," that is, queer migration studies. Through an analysis of (im-) mobile sexualities in Mohamed Abdulkarim Ali's *Angry Queer Somali Boy* (2019), I claim that queer refugee narratives present a transcultural existence at the intersection of local and global that denounces monolithic identities and the official gender regime of nation-states reinforced and protected by state control mechanisms. The memoir shows that while refugee women are obliged to become the carriers of national values and the heteropatriarchal system, queerness challenges, destroys, and disrupts these impositions through its transgression of various boundaries. Consequently, queer refugee world-making as a narrative form also undermines the boundaries of national literature and nation-making projects, asserting its presence within the broader global literary space.

***

Introduction

The primary structure of national imaginaries, which operates on binary terms such as citizens versus foreigners, still defines the figure of 'proper' migrants using heterosexual and patriarchal terms. The state's control mechanisms (such as the police force, immigration control systems, and surveillance mechanisms) protect, reproduce, and reinforce these hetero-patriarchal gender roles and normative sexual identities. Hence, queer refugees are pushed to the margins of national affinity. In this chapter, sexuality serves as the analytical lens through which I approach nationalism and mobility, as I explore what Eithne Luibhéid calls the "unruly body of inquiry" (Luibhéid 2008, 169), namely queer migration studies. This chapter is a result of numerous meaningful discussions and equally significant readings that were delved into during 2022 while preparing for my dissertation. Through an analysis of (im-)mobile sexualities, Mohamed Abdulkarim Ali's *Angry Queer Somali Boy* (2019) shows that queer refugee narratives present a transcultural existence at the intersection of local and global, which ultimately denounces monolithic identities and the official gender regime of nation-states reinforced and protected by domestic and international control mechanisms. Consequently, queer refugee world-making as a narrative form also undermines the boundaries of national literature and nation-making projects, asserting its presence within the broader global literary space.

This chapter begins with an analytical framework defining the key terms, namely, refugee, queerness, and migration. The definition of these concepts paves the way for understanding how nation-making practices affect sexuality and movement. Next, the chapter continues with an analysis of the memoir, focusing first on Samira, Mohamed Abdulkarim Ali's stepmother. Samira's characterization presents a palpable showcase of women's relation to nationhood while challenging the conventional patriarchal family dynamic. Later, it analyzes the impossibilities that Ali faces due to hetero-patriarchal and national borders before it moves onto Ali's way of creating possibilities through Internet cruising and performing *hajj*. Finally, the chapter asserts the global importance of queer refugee narratives as a conscious deviation from the nation-building apparatus, including national literature.

Theoretical Framework

Life writing, as Phillippe Lejeune suggests, is "personal, individual, and simple" (Lejeune 1989, 149). These very generalized restrictions of the genre emphasize the importance of the first-person perspective or the 'I.' However, Julie Rak reminds us that memoirs are not just about an individual's collection of memories. Memoirs mark the ways in which private lives become part of public discourse, emphasizing how individual lives are shaped by, and in turn shape, larger societal forces (Rak 2013, 6). It unravels how life writing never exists in isolation; instead, it transpires as a certain mediation between the self and society (Minich 2015, 60). In the case of queer refugee memoirs, the signified (representation of queer refugees) and the signifier (public discourse on queer refugees) are finally produced by the same person. This allows for a recovery of agency and a juncture between being acted upon and acting through the narrative. In this sense, a memoir is a medium of social commentary and resistance, as well as a translation of personal trauma. Through the queer refugee framework, this chapter situates memoir as both an individual and collective act of worldmaking. As Y-Dang Troeung describes, "refugee worldmaking" is a creative process through which refugees reconstruct their identities and worlds in response to the violence of forced migration (Troeung 2021, 10). Ali's worldmaking with this memoir illustrates the tension between mobility and immobility through its focus on nation-state borders, sexuality, and entrapped identity between diaspora, heterosexuality, and whiteness. Additionally, Ali's transnational movement and its textual explorations in this memoir emerge as a form of defiance against national boundaries, whether it is material or literary.

Although this memoir shares valuable insights into the intersections of queerness, mobility, and sexuality, one of the limitations of this paper comes from its focus on only one memoir on queer refugee experience. This singular focus runs the risk of overlooking the diversity and multiplicity of queer refugee voices, and by focusing on Ali's memoir alone, this paper risks generalizing his specific experiences to all queer refugees. However, although individual experiences and circumstances shift and vary, the systems of oppression operate in a common and repeated pattern. This chapter aims to highlight these broader patterns of institutionalized and systemic oppression by focusing on movement and sexuality. The singular focus of Ali's memoir allows for an in-depth and comprehensive examination of these layers of systematic violence and oppression.

The book begins with the consciousness of recovered agency and explicitly disclaims that it "is about addiction and recovery from trauma" (Ali 2019, vii). It opens with a description of Ali's birthplace, Mogadishu, Somalia, which was ravaged by the civil war at the time. Ali's father takes him away from his birth mother to bring him to Abu Dhabi to live with his stepmother, Samira, and three step-siblings. Ali and his new family later seek refuge in the Netherlands. After a long process of struggling to assimilate into the Dutch system, the family moves once again, this time to Toronto. Ali embarks on a journey of self-discovery as a queer Somali boy in Toronto while grappling with mental health and addiction problems. In the meantime, he must endure Samira's mental and physical abuse. After a suicide attempt, Ali comes out to Samira, who tries to ship Ali back to Somalia for an arranged marriage. Ali escapes this plan and, as a result, cuts ties with his family. At the end of the book, Ali expresses that he is writing this memoir from a men's shelter in Toronto, as he does not have employment or residence.

This analysis begins with several foundational questions to establish the conceptual framework: When does a refugee cease to be a refugee? Is it when the government grants permanent residence or when the claimant receives a new passport? How about queerness? When does a person become queer? Is it when they come out of the closet for the first time or start pursuing their queer desires? These questions, unfortunately, do not yield simple answers; however, they lead to a broader realization that queerness and refugeeness are both ontologically (re-)constructed within changing social, political and cultural contexts. Consequently, the legal framework legitimizing exclusion and normalizing surveillance and discipline through rigid labels such as asylum seekers, refugees, and stateless people is extraneous for this chapter. Vihn Nguyen's theorization of refugeetude, which "describes a coming into consciousness of the forces that produce and structure 'refuge' and 'refugee' is followed. It names the forms of recognition, articulation, and relation that emerge from the experience of refuge(e), as well as the attempts to redefine and live it differently from what the legal framework—as contemporary arbiter of refugee lives—allows" (Nguyen 2019, 110). Refugeetude –like negritude or migritude– can function as a new consciousness that holds the potential to claim agency over oppression and marginalization; a consciousness that affirms belonging to a certain nation requires more than citizenship status. Refugeetude informs how this study approaches queer refugee narratives, as it has the potential to operate beyond legal and bureaucratic terms. Refugeetude blurs the line between terms such as 'immigrant' and 'refugee,' like the daily realities of refugees like Mohamed Adbulkarim Ali. Similar to the refugeetude definition, the use of the term 'queer' also problematizes rigid categorizations of sexualities, since it suggests a fluid transgression of borders of all sorts. The term "queer" in this study is used similarly to Eithne Luibhéid's use of the term as "a call to transform, rather than to seek accommodation within, existing structures" (Luibhéid 2005, x). This definition facilitates a constructive approach to migration research beyond normative rationales.

An influential scholar in queer migration field, Eithne Luibhéid, starts her book *Entry Denied* by acknowledging the importance of Foucault's work on migration studies (Luibhéid 2002, xiv–xv). Foucault's body of work remains relevant to migration studies since his theory of sexuality and its historical implications on governance still contribute to the theorization of how migrant bodies are disciplined and controlled. According to him, the calculated management of life was particularly involved with sexuality, as "on the one hand, it was tied to discipline of the body…on the other hand, it applied to the regulation of populations" (Foucault [1978] 1990, 145). The expansion of power to discipline and manage populations occurs through the transformation of sex into discourse; therefore, analysis of such power requires an examination of the multiple sites where normalization occurs through discourse and knowledge production (Foucault [1978] 1990, 61; 89–90). Following Foucault's footsteps, Lionel Cantú (2009) emphasizes "one such site of normalization is immigration and all its entanglements" (Cantú 2009, 34). In light of this, sexuality and mobility as sites of normalization not only discipline the nation but also function across transnational borders and within the heteropatriarchal system.

Benedict Anderson (2006) considers nations as imagined communities formed through historical processes, reinforced by rituals, beliefs, and cultural artifacts (Anderson 2006, 4). This imagined community is delimited by certain borders, which reinforce a unified and homogeneous national identity and sovereignty. These imaginary borders designate a sense of belonging, or rather, unbelonging, to civilians depending on their race, ethnicity, gender, and sexuality. Border control – formulated as a mechanism that emphasizes the otherness of the imagined Other – exerts its control over migrant bodies by determining what is appropriate inside the borders in terms of gender, sexuality, race, and religion through judicial power. For example, granting protection to refugee claims based on sexual orientation or gender identity (SOGI) is a relatively recent addition to Canada's refugee policy, despite being one of the first countries to do so (Jordan and Morrissey 2013, 13). The border reproduces reproductive and patriarchal heterosexuality as its official sexual and gender order (Luibhéid 2002, xviii). Consequently, border crossing mobility becomes the very first passage to challenge the reciprocal relationship between nation and heterosexuality. It also provides a vantage point for this paper's analysis of queerness in motion. In light of this, Samira, as an unconventional refugee woman, and Ali, as an eternally angry queer Somali boy, occupy the focus of this paper. Although both heterosexual women and queer men are subjugated by national heteropatriarchy through societal exclusion, they diverge in how they are controlled at the borders.

This divergence also takes precedence in mobility studies, as scholars continue to debate what constitutes queer migration. Andrew Gorman-Murray declares that queer migration only "occurs when the needs or desires of non-heterosexual identities, practices and performances are implicated in the process of displacement, influencing the decision to leave a certain place or choose a particular destination" (Murray 2009, 443). In other words, Gorman-Murray suggests that queer migration can only carry the identifier "queer" if the subject is crossing the border on the basis of sexual orientation and gender identity; not for other political, economic, or cultural reasons. Unfortunately, Gorman-Murray's strict gatekeeping of the broad scope of queer migration reproduces the legal and political restrictions that hover over queer refugees on a daily basis. In this sense, these rigid distinctions legitimize the denial of entry for at-risk refugees (queer or not) while normalizing the surveillance and disciplining of their bodies. Relevantly, the case of *Angry Queer Somali Boy* complicates such frigid definitions of queer migration throughout the memoir because Mohamed Abdulkarim Ali's border crossing activities – until the very end – do not occur because of his sexuality. Although he is queer and migrant, his mobility falls outside of Gorman-Murray's definition of queer migration, and therefore it is transposed as a figurative immobility. Ali's queerness and mobility prove to be "unruly" as they pose a constant negotiation even within the field of queer migration.

Family Dynamics In Flux: Samira

In the memoir, Ali's migration is initiated by his father in an effort to save him from the unsafe environment in Somalia. After a while, the situation in Abu Dhabi also proves to be dangerous for Ali's family, and his father decides to send the family away to London, saying, "These Arabs are heartless. London, take it or leave it" (Ali 2019, 15). Forced to cross the borders, Samira, her three children, and Ali set out for London, leaving his father in Abu Dhabi. Samira declares her independence from patriarchal and national control at the airport and decides to go to Schiphol, the Netherlands' main international airport, instead of London. The moment Samira crosses national borders, she is marked as a symbol of her culture and nation, with the obligation to keep alive the nostalgic dream of going back home. In Women-Nation-State (1989), Floya Anthias and Nira Yuval Davis articulate how women engage with ethnic and national processes (Anthias and Davis 1989, 6–7). Not only are women biological reproducers of a nation, but they are also seen as "cultural carriers" of an ethnic group. They "teach and transfer" the rituals, beliefs, and cultural artifacts of their imagined community (Anthias and Davis 1989, 9). As the emblem of an ethnic group, they are also tasked with the protection and reproduction of imagined boundaries. Because of Samira's impositions, Ali has to do well in school to return to Somalia: "In essence, we forewent any sense of self in our new homes so that we might go back and fix a country they fucked up in the first place" (Ali 2019, 71–72).

This act of border crossing disrupts the heterosexual and patriarchal family dynamics where the father is mobile and out of the home, while the mother is eternally trapped and immobilized. Instead, Ali's father is associated with inertia in Abu Dhabi, and Samira becomes autonomous and mobile, posing a threat and a site of instability to national heteronormativity. Consequently, the national proliferation of heterosexuality and patriarchal power loses its dominance over Samira and Ali alike once the family starts to function on a transnational dynamic, leaving the father's control behind. Ali distinctly remembers one incident when his father called Samira a whore, "she beat him...she walked to the front door and locked it from the inside...For the next ten minutes, he begged her to stop...He couldn't face us and I was happy at seeing him hurt. He got a slice of what I endured" (Ali 2019, 40). As a result, he states his father "was no hero," and he "lost all confidence in my [his] father" (Ali 2019, 38). Ali connects Samira's continuous violence first to her newfound independence, as she has now become the head of the family and therefore wields the tools of patriarchal oppression. As the secondary factor to her violence, Ali identifies the feeling of alienation due to migration. He explains that violence becomes a way of expressing her frustrations, as she struggles to adapt to the unfamiliar environment while fiercely protecting the remnants of her cultural identity. She faces challenges with establishing social connections and navigating the responsibilities of being a single mother, all while dealing with financial problems, which exacerbate her violent behavior.

Trapped in Transit: Mohamed

While Samira becomes more mobile as the head of the family upon refuge, Ali is stuck, i.e., immobile, between various tangents such as the Somali diaspora and the host community, heterosexual biological family and mobile queer desires, and Westernization and Islam. Ali's first dilemma is the association of queerness with whiteness in the Somali diaspora. For example, Ali's sister Fadumo likes watching white gay men on TV and expresses her desire to become friends with them. Ali decodes what Fadumo implies to the reader: "What she meant was that homosexuality in white bodies was acceptable. As a Somali, I disgraced our heritage. Queerness was a fine complement to the Western degeneracy we inhabited, yet in our Islamic culture, it was a symptom of sickness" (Ali 2019, 135). This portrayal of queerness is surely not limited to the Somali diaspora, in fact, the homonationalist discourse as an imperial tool "repeatedly coheres whiteness as a queer norm and straightness as a racial norm" (Puar 2017, xxxii). Then, Ali's detachment from Somali diaspora signals double marginalization within a predominantly white host society where queerness is often racialized as white, and within Somali diaspora, where queerness is stigmatized as a symptom of Western corruption.

Constantly feeling isolated from the diaspora, Ali defines his identity through movement and calls himself the "wanderer" (Ali 2019, 74) even though his mobility is strictly controlled, forced, and blocked. The immobility illustrates how, despite numerous years of resettlement processes, Ali's identity is shaped significantly by his refugee background. That is why Ali's struggles can only be understood through the lens of refugeetude. Ali's immobility is not just physical, but also socio-cultural, as he remains caught between sexual, racial, and financial impositions. He struggles with economic precarity, exploitation, and alienation, all of which hinder the sense of belonging and incite a constant flux in Ali's life.

For example, the family's future, including Ali's, is almost predetermined due to the lack of opportunities available to refugees, starting with the family's residence in a refugee-populated ghetto with limited opportunities for social integration and economic prosperity. The infamous neighborhood of Jane and Finch in Toronto, which "suffered from the usual social ills associated with diverse and poor neighbourhoods" (Ali 2019, 70), is strictly under police surveillance and control. The residents are "more concerned about the police than the criminals or gun violence" because the police "rode up and down the neighbourhood and made their presence felt" (Ali 2019, 79). Coming from Jane and Finch, Ali "couldn't vibe with most of the other white students" as "[t]hey led lives that I [Ali] watched on TV. They knew nothing of the ghetto beyond what they saw on TV" (Ali 2019, 116). The ghetto is not only heavily and systematically disenfranchised, but it is also heavily surveilled as a population control mechanism and actively excluded from social relations. This sense of confinement, limited resources, domestic violence, and an ever-growing feeling of unbelonging leads Ali to drugs as a coping mechanism: "I coped with a diminished sense of self by diving, headfirst, into the world of drugs" (Ali 2019, 59).

Unpacking Anger and Happiness

Ali's unbelonging results in anger and unhappiness as hinted at in the title of the memoir. According to Sara Ahmed, the unhappy migrant is an affected alien –a condition of being "out of line with the public mood, not to feel the way others feel in response to an event" (Ahmed 2010, 157). Happiness as a form of world-making not only determines the "good" subject, but also aligns it with the norm. Migrants are particularly charged with "the happiness duty" in multicultural nation-states (such as Canada) because, as would-be citizens, they are required to let go of the pain of racism in the host country and liberate themselves from suffering by becoming happy – in other words, "civilized" (Ahmed 2010, 130). If a migrant fails to integrate, they pose a threat to national happiness, because the multicultural image of Canada is dependent on the active – and yet controlled – participation of racialized immigrants and refugees. Ali's dark humor points out racialized police violence and surveillance as mentioned above and animated cheerful diversity in Toronto: "Toronto's motto is diversity is our strength. What is more diverse than black flesh on a police baton!" (Ali 2019, 79). This observation demonstrates how, underneath multiculturalism's colorful and cheerful façade, monolithic Canadian national identity maintains whiteness as the "norm" and reinforces its supremacy over immigrants through state-sanctioned violence.

The happiness duty helps frame Ali's family dynamics. As the queer son of a Muslim family, he fails to "inherit" the heterosexual family as his happy object. Sara Ahmed states that queer people are always associated with the cause of unhappiness because of their inability to inherit compulsory heterosexuality, and thus they are made unhappy in return (Ahmed 2010, 97–98). His "failure" to comply with the patriarchal and heterosexual family structure as a gay man prompts Samira, the carrier of these values, to use a myriad of violent tactics to make Ali unhappy. When Ali falls in love with a Dutch boy named Caspar in the

Netherlands, Samira decides to move again before Ali can pursue this love interest. Considering how this move affects his sexual desires, Ali says, "I didn't realize it then, but this is a tactic abusers use to keep their hostages isolated. She wanted to control our connection to the outside" (Ali 2019, 56). As the violent and persistent protector of the ethnic and familial boundaries, Samira controls Ali's sexuality in a similar way to how borders control the official sexuality regime of the nation. Public and private borders act as barriers that render Ali's queer desires impossible. While mobility can serve as a catalyst for exploring one's sexuality, it can also hinder and restrict sexual expression, as Ali's life story illustrates. Later in the memoir, when Ali comes out of the closet, his sexuality is so violently rejected by Samira that he attempts suicide.

Ali's happiness duty is also tied to a homonormative rationale that propagates the "migration to liberation nation" narrative for queer migrants (Murray 2014, 452). In such narratives, the refugee-receiving nation is acknowledged as a civilized and queer-friendly society, as opposed to "'uncivilized' societies characterized by their rampant homophobia" (Murray 2014, 453). This popular trope, perpetuated by many Western countries, becomes a legitimate civilizing mission and a justification for the discrimination of racialized migrants under the guise of tolerance. Ali becomes acutely aware of such hypocrisy as a Bachelor student at Ryerson when he comes out to his university friends: "My new friends at Ryerson, a pastiche of Canadian multicultural policy, feigned indifference or ran.... They befriended someone who ate bootyholes. *Poor ghetto youth, free your mind!*" (Ali 2019, 125; italics in the original). The part in italics indicates how the citizens of multicultural nation-states perpetuate Islamophobia by positioning Muslim and racialized immigrants as uncivilized, backward, or generally unmannered. However, the reaction that Ali gets when he comes out to his middle-class Canadian friends reveals how queerness becomes the apparatus to discipline, control, and "civilize" the poor ghetto youth and normalize the exclusion of those racialized and foreign others. Ali's subject position and sexuality are perceived as abject: something to be controlled, disciplined, or exerted. This dynamic of abjection operates within the broader framework of homonationalism, where queerness is co-opted into the national project to reinforce the hierarchy of the West. The expectation within this framework is that Ali serves to maintain the myth of Canada as a multicultural and queer-friendly society by sweeping his abjection under the carpet.

Transgressing Borders: Queer (Im)Mobility

This abjection is integral to the border regime that, as Sonny Dhoot notes, is one of the sites where Canadian homonationalism performs "an interpellative function for homonormative subjects" where "inclusion and celebration of some im/migrants while maintaining strict border controls against migrants marked as 'threats'" (Dhoot 2017, 53). Unfortunately, Ali also experiences discrimination at the airport, as he is perceived as a threat at the border. After Ali comes out of the closet, he is exiled from the heterosexual family home when Samira decides to ship Ali back to Somalia via London for an arranged marriage. After spending six weeks in London, Ali gets to Gatwick Airport to make an escape to Toronto. This marks Ali's first and last queer migration that fits into Gorman-Murray's definition. However, Ali faces a second risk of exile at transnational borders since homonationalism systems of nation-states function to deport, expel, and disperse the racialized refugee:

> At Gatwick Airport, I felt secure enough to sit down...I could fast-track you, sir. If you don't mind stepping over here, please.
>
> I smiled and pretended not to hear him.
>
> If you cooperate sir, this will go a lot smoother.
>
> He read the confusion in my face.
>
> You've been selected randomly for a security check. Could I see your passport?
>
> ...Why was I being treated with such suspicion? I wanted to be free. (Ali 2019, 149–50)

Travelling as a racialized single man, Ali is suddenly a threat, a "terrorist-look-alike" as Dhoot calls it, rather than a migrant in need of liberation (Dhoot 2017, 52). As Puar reminds us, this is part of the homonationalist matrix of affects, which mines "any evidence of non-assimilative behavior" through racial profiling or border control technologies to mark "for death in the name of national life-making" (Puar 2017, 161; Dhoot 2017, 51). Once Ali lands in Toronto, he is again singled out by immigration officials. After spending four hours in a windowless room at Pearson Airport, the immigration officials finally decide that he is not a security risk. Ali reflects on the hypocrisy of homonationalist politics in Canada by saying: "Canada, and the other white societies of the West, want us immigrants to be loyal and willing to die for their democracies yet see no hypocrisy in treating us as suspects" (Ali 2019, 150). The ontological reality of queerness and refugeetude painfully swings between inertia and movement, control and liberation.

While Ali's body is controlled and disciplined across physical borders, leading to mobility restrictions, the Internet provides a borderless space for the freedom of his queer desires. Cyberspace provides a myriad of sexual possibilities in which online and offline worlds intertwine: "The Internet was crucial to my cruising, or the act of finding dick. I went to a far-off computer lab and used any of the streetcar lines or subway stations that crisscrossed the campus to get to Sherbourne, Queen, Dundas, Bleecker, Wellesley, Bay, and so on" (Ali 2019, 126). Consequently, the Internet allows for a re-mapping of the city through the lens of sexual desires; the online list of "dicks" not only informs but also rearranges the offline movement of Ali. This imagined relation between online cartographies and offline geographies undermines the sites of normalization in Ali's life, namely the borders of nation-states and the heterosexual family structure. Mark Turner, writing about queer cruising through the city, states "the Internet is a medium that challenges fundamentally the significance of conventional borders and boundaries, of concepts like the nation-state itself" (Turner 2003, 173). Despite being highly corporatized, cyberspace serves as a form of global deterritorialization of the aforementioned private and public borders that render queer sexuality an impossibility. Instead, it allows for a transgression of borders and creates new possibilities for queer relations.

Aside from its potential to undermine borders, the Internet becomes a safer outlet for Ali's non-normative desires and sexualities. As mentioned previously, the unthinkability of a queer Muslim within various mappings of the nation and diaspora results in an unsafe environment for Ali (Gopinath 2005, 10). Nicola Do¨ring notes that the internet is an essential place of refuge "for individuals who do not have access to urban subcultures by virtue of social restrictions" (Do¨ring 2009, 1097). The act of "finding dick" online is both a necessary refuge and a mechanism of subversion simply due to his inability to access queer spaces and people, as well as the impossibility of being openly queer in his family and diaspora.

At the end of the memoir, Ali cuts all his ties to his connections, family, diasporic community, and friends. Jobless, he lives in a men's homeless shelter in Toronto. In a way, losing everything in his life is a reset to the trauma of national heteropatriarchy and queer impossibilities. In an effort to mark the ending of impossibilities in his life and initiate a peaceful start into his new life, Ali decides to walk around the city where most of the memories of his past life are located: "The next day I decided I was going to perform a pilgrimage, or hajj as Muslims called it. I had come so close to dying. No one in my past would've known of my death. I felt unmoored from reality and needed to remember that I existed at some point" (Ali 2019, 185). This time, his mobility is not to defy the obstacles around him, nor is it to escape violence. Rather, it is an effort to belong, even when it is belonging in flux; it is a struggle towards acceptance, not acceptance of society, but an acceptance of the self. He hints at a possibility of a reset to the trauma of national heteropatriarchy and queer impossibilities when he says, "By going on this journey, I wanted to liberate myself from the shackles of the past" (Ali 2019, 185). Although the memoir concludes without a happy ending, I posit that this final movement permits a hopeful rendition. It insinuates healing, signifying the restoration of agency that was systematically stripped away from Ali. As a queer Somali refugee, he finds a juncture between being acted upon and acting in his movements which locates him in both online and offline spaces across the globe. Ali's hajj becomes an indicator of a transcultural belonging, a future full of queer possibilities while sustaining movement across borders. His refugeetude and queerness transform into ways of understanding the interconnectedness of the world beyond the national and heteronormative boundaries.

Reflecting on the Global Literary Space

So far, this chapter has examined how nation-making structures propagate violence against queer refugees through an analysis of mobility and sexuality in the memoir. It was also established how state-sanctioned and domestic violence incite feelings of (im-)possibility and unbelonging for Ali throughout the book. However, one question remains: What are the implications of such works for literary studies? Firstly, Ali's work stands outside of national and diasporic literatures (namely Dutch, Canadian, Somali, and Arabic) since Ali repeatedly declares his unbelonging to these national affinities. Ali appears as an alien in these communities, much like this work, which stands distinctly outside of national literary categories. This memoir is a narration of movements, and hence, it defines itself through movement. This poses a resistance to prominent literary categories by overflowing, being multiple in one.

As mentioned earlier in the chapter, by externalizing the private self into public discourse, queer refugee writers create a fictional world that complements the biographical one. Y-Dang Troeung refers to this creation as refugee worldmaking, defined as "reparative acts of creativity that refugees deploy to remake themselves and their worlds" (Troeung 2021, 10). This act of creation sheds light on the interconnected systems of imperial, racial, and gendered violence that actively create and shape the material realities of refugees (Troeung 2021, 11). I consider queer refugee worldmaking as an effort to collectively deviate from nation-making practices, institutions, and cultural artifacts. It is a collection of narratives that leads to a deeper understanding of refugee and queer experiences across cultures while asserting its presence within the broader global literary space. Queer refugee worldmaking becomes "worldly" – as opposed to monolithic or uniform qualities of national literatures – through its ability to simultaneously capture the dynamic realities of globalization and accelerated border-crossing movements while subverting exclusionary practices. Additionally, queer refugee narratives shift the meaning of worldly existence from a state of being commonly associated with the elite frequent flyer businessperson to an ordinary existence of many subalterns like migrants, refugees, asylees, workers, and queers. This analysis, then, calls for an acknowledgement of the state-sanctioned violence of borders, legal categories, and heteronormativity. It is also a call for solidarity and resistance beyond these oppressive systems through narrative and movement.

Conclusion

This analysis of *Angry Queer Somali Boy* tries to demonstrate that "unruly" works of literature challenge the controlling mechanisms of nation-states and their official sexuality and gender order. While Samira reverses the oppressive patriarchal family dynamic through mobility, Ali's experience is multi-faceted. Even though the heteropatriarchal violence and nation-state oppression renders Ali immobile or forcefully migrated, he transgresses restrictions to find queer possibilities. Ali's expressions of sexuality and queer desires enable the readers to examine the ways in which sexuality informs and alters mobility. Ultimately, Ali's movement becomes a marker of new possibilities that could be stripped of the violence of the heterosexual family, trauma of unbelonging, and dehumanizing processes of control and disciplining migrant bodies. Additionally, Ali's memoir demonstrates how queer refugee worldmaking enables the transnational movement of narratives while effectively undermining the constraints of nation-making projects, including national literature.

References

Ahmed, Sara. *The Promise of Happiness*. Durham and London: Duke University Press, 2010.

Ali, Mohamed Abdulkarim. *Angry Queer Somali Boy: A Complicated Memoir*. The Regina Collection. Saskatchewan, Canada: University of Regina Press, 2019. https://doi.org/10.1515/9780889776609

Anderson, Benedict. *Imagined Communities: Reflections on the Origin and Spread of Nationalism*. Revised Edition. London: Verso, 2006.

Cantú, Lionel. *The Sexuality of Migration: Border Crossings and Mexican Immigrant Men*. New York: New York University Press, 2009.

Dhoot, Sonny. "Homonationalism and Failure to Interpellate." In *The Psychic Life of Racism in Gay Men's Communities*, edited by Damien W. Riggs, 49–65. Lanham: Lexington Books, 2017. https://doi.org/10.5771/9781498537155-49

Döring, Nicola M. "The Internet's Impact on Sexuality: A Critical Review of 15 Years of Research." *Computers in Human Behavior* 25, no. 5 (2009): 1089–1101. https://doi.org/10.1016/j.chb.2009.04.003.

Foucault, Michel. *The History of Sexuality, Volume 1: An Introduction*. Vintage Books edition. Originally published in 1978. New York: Vintage Books, 1990.

Gopinath, Gayatri. *Impossible Desires: Queer Diasporas and South Asian Public Cultures*. Perverse Modernities. Durham: Duke University Press, 2005. https://doi.org/10.2307/j.ctv11smg4c

Gorman-Murray, Andrew. "Intimate Mobilities: Emotional Embodiment and Queer Migration." *Social & Cultural Geography* 10, no. 4 (2009): 441–60. https://doi.org/10.1080/14649360902853262.

Jordan, Sharalyn, and Chris Morrissey. "'On What Grounds?' LGBT Asylum Claims in Canada." *Forced Migration Review*, no. 42 (April 2013): 13–15. https://www.fmreview.org/sites/fmr/files/FMRdownloads/en/sogi/jordan-morrissey.pdf.

Lejeune, Philippe. *On Autobiography*. Minneapolis: University of Minnesota Press, 1989.

Luibhéid, Eithne. *Entry Denied: Controlling Sexuality at the Border*. Minneapolis: University of Minnesota Press, 2002.

———. "Introduction: Queering Migration and Citizenship." In *Queer Migrations: Sexuality, U.S. Citizenship, and Border Crossings*, edited by Lionel Cantú and Eithne Luibhéid, New Edition, ix–xvi. University of Minnesota Press, 2005. http://www.jstor.org/stable/10.5749/j.ctttt4g7.4 .

———. "Queer/Migration: An Unruly Body of Scholarship." *GLQ: A Journal of Lesbian and Gay Studies* 14, no. 2–3 (2008): 169–90. https://doi.org/10.1215/10642684-2007-029.

Minich, Julie Avril. "Writing Queer Lives: Autobiography and Memoir." In *The Cambridge Companion to American Gay and Lesbian Literature*, edited by Scott Herring, 59–72. Cambridge, United Kingdom: Cambridge University Press, 2015. http://www.proquest.com/docview/2137996318/citation/4A6F744C9946ACPQ/1. https://doi.org/10.1017/CCO9781107110250.006

Murray, David AB. "The (Not so) Straight Story: Queering Migration Narratives of Sexual Orientation and Gendered Identity Refugee Claimants." *Sexualities* 17, no. 4 (2014): 451–71. https://doi.org/10.1177/1363460714524767.

Nguyen, Vinh. "Refugeetude: When Does a Refugee Stop Being a Refugee?" *Social Text* 37, no. 2 (2019): 109–31. https://doi.org/10.1215/01642472-7371003.

Puar, Jasbir K. *Terrorist Assemblages: Homonationalism in Queer Times*. Tenth anniversary expanded edition. Durham: Duke University Press, 2017.

Rak, Julie. *Boom: Manufacturing Memoir for the Popular Market*. Waterloo, ON: Wilfrid Laurier University Press, 2013.

Troeung, Y.-Dang. "On Refugee Worldmaking." *Canadian Literature*, no. 246 (2021): 6–14. https://www.proquest.com/docview/2630320889/abstract/B919B581915D4D7CPQ/1.

Turner, Mark W. *Backward Glances: Cruising the Queer Streets of New York and London*. London: Reaktion, 2003.

Yuval-Davis, Nira, and Floya Anthias. "Introduction." In *Woman, Nation, State*, 1–15. New York: St. Martin's Press, 1989.

Chapter Three
Unveiling the Embodied Nexus: Interrogating the Interplay of Queer and Crip Identities in the Cinematic Landscape of *Margarita with a Straw*

Avijit Pramanik
Ramkrishna Mahato Government Engineering College, Purulia

Abstract

This chapter critically engages with the intersection of queer and crip identities as portrayed in the film *Margarita with a Straw*. Through an in-depth analysis of the film's narrative, characters, and cinematic techniques, this study explores how the film navigates the complexities of queerness and disability, challenging traditional notions of identity, sexuality, and bodily autonomy. Drawing on queer theory and disability studies, this research examines the nuanced portrayal of the protagonist, Laila, a young woman with cerebral palsy, as she embarks on a journey of self-discovery and sexual exploration. By employing a multidimensional approach, this study examines how Laila's queerness intersects with her disability, shaping her experiences, relationships, and sense of self. The analysis delves into the film's portrayal of Laila's relationships, both romantic and platonic, highlighting the intricate ways in which her disability and queerness intersect and influence her interactions with others. Furthermore, this research examines the film's depiction of Laila's personal struggles, desires, and agency, shedding light on the challenges she faced in reconciling her multiple identities within a heteronormative and ableist society. In addition to exploring the narrative and character development, this study closely examines the film's visual and auditory elements, uncovering how cinematography, sound design, and mise-en-scène contribute to the representation of queer and crip experiences. By analyzing the film's aesthetic choices, this chapter aims to reveal the cinematic techniques employed to challenge and subvert dominant narratives surrounding queerness and disability. Ultimately, this study contributes to the broader discourse on the intersectionality of queer and crip identities within the realm of film. By examining *Margarita with a Straw* as a case study, this chapter offers insights into the complexities, contradictions, and potentials of representing diverse identities on screen. The findings of this research expand our understanding of the ways in which queerness and disability intersect, prompting a critical reevaluation of societal norms and challenging the limitations imposed upon marginalized individuals.

Keywords: Queer, Disability, Intersectionality, Heteronormativity, Ableism, Inclusion

***

Introduction

Queer studies and crip studies have emerged as vital areas of academic inquiry and activism, each focused on illuminating the lived experiences of marginalized communities and challenging societal norms. While they address different aspects of identity—one centered on sexual orientation and gender, the other on disability—they share compelling commonalities that warrant deeper examination. One of the salient commonalities between queer studies and crip studies is their recognition of the intersectionality of identity. Both fields contend that individuals do not exist within isolated identity categories but rather inhabit multiple, often intersecting, identities that shape their experiences. Queer individuals, for example, may also identify as disabled, leading to unique experiences that neither field can fully capture in isolation. Recognizing these intersections enables a more nuanced understanding of the lives and struggles of marginalized individuals. Both disciplines are united in their mission to challenge normative paradigms and dismantle oppressive structures. Queer studies have long sought to disrupt the binary notions of gender and sexuality, while crip studies call into question the ableist assumptions that underlie societal definitions of "normalcy." An examination of normalcy plays a pivotal role in the disability rights movement and within the field of disability studies, as exemplified by Lennard Davis's comprehensive analysis and critique of the historical evolution of "normalcy" (Davis 1995) or Rosemarie Garland-Thomson's introduction of the term "normate" (Thomson 1997). This shared goal of deconstructing normative frameworks leads to a fruitful exchange of ideas and methodologies, fostering a more comprehensive critique of societal power structures. Eli Clare rightly comments that "*Queer* and *Cripple* are cousins: words to shock, words to infuse with pride and self-love, words to resist internalized hatred, words to help forge a politics. They have been gladly chosen—*queer* by many gay/lesbian/trans people, *cripple*, or *crip*, by many disabled people" (Clare 1999, 70).

Queer studies and crip studies prioritize centering the lived experiences of individuals, giving voice to those who have historically been silenced or marginalized. McRuer argues that "[l]ike 'queer,' 'crip' has been a pejorative word that has been reclaimed by the very people it was meant to wound. Derived in English from 'cripple,' 'crip' has been used as a more radical and defiant word than disability over the past few decades, similar to the ways in which queer has been used by LGBT people" (McRuer 2017, 139). Queer theory emphasizes the importance of personal narratives and storytelling in challenging heteronormative ideologies. Similarly, the context of crip studies promotes disability narratives to be heard and respected, highlighting the value of experiential knowledge in understanding disability. Both fields are deeply engaged in activist endeavors, advocating for social justice and inclusion. Activists within the queer and disabled communities often find themselves collaborating on issues such as accessible healthcare, equal rights, and representation in media. These collaborations strengthen the collective impact of both movements, fostering a sense of solidarity among marginalized groups. Jeffrey Escoffier and Allan Berubé observed that "queer" gave birth to a politics that was "meant to be confrontational – opposed to gay assimilationists and straight oppressors while inclusive of people who have been marginalized by anyone in power" (Escoffier and Berubé 1991, 4). Queer studies and crip studies also recognize the fluidity of identity and the ways in which individuals may move in and out of categories and labels. This fluidity challenges rigid definitions and encourages a more dynamic and inclusive approach to understanding identity. Reflecting this focus on adaptability and diversity, Eve Kosofsky Sedgwick observed, as expressed in a frequently cited passage from her essay "Queer and Now," that the term "queer" has the potential to signify a broad range of identities:

> The experimental linguistic, epistemological, representational, political adventures attaching to the very many of us who may at times be moved to describe ourselves as (among many other possibilities) pushy femmes, radical faeries, fantasists, drags, clones, leatherfolk, ladies in tuxedos, feminist women or feminist men, masturbators, bulldaggers, divas, Snap! Queens, butch bottoms, storytellers, transsexuals, aunties, wannabes, lesbian-identified men or lesbians who sleep with men, or…people able to relish, learn from, or identify with such. (Sedgwick 1983, 8)

In alignment with this empowering concept of queerness, Lennard Davis contends that, in modern society, the autonomy of bodies remains a distant aspiration, as all citizens are fundamentally interdependent. In his *Bending over Backwards: Disability, Dismodernism, and Other Difficult Positions*, Davis argues that:

This new way of thinking, which I am calling dismodernism, rests on the operative notion that postmodernism is still based on a humanistic model. Politics have been directed toward making all identities equal under a model of the rights of the dominant, often white, male, "normal" subject. In a dismodernist mode, the ideal is not a hypostatization of the normal (that is, dominant) subject, but aims to create a new category based on the partial, incomplete subject whose realization is not autonomy and independence but dependency and interdependence... The dismodernist subject is, in fact, disabled, only completed by technology and by interventions. (Davis 2002, 30)

Queer studies and crip studies, while rooted in distinct experiences, ideologies, and histories, converge in profound and significant ways. Their shared emphasis on intersectionality, the deconstruction of norms, the validation of lived experience, intersectional activism, and recognition of identity fluidity creates a fertile ground for collaboration and mutual enrichment. By recognizing these commonalities, scholars and activists can work together to advance social justice, inclusivity, and the dismantling of oppressive structures that affect both queer and disabled communities. The synergy between these disciplines has the potential to be a powerful force in reshaping our understanding of identity and liberation.

This chapter explores the intricate convergence of queerness and disability as depicted in the 2015 film *Margarita with a Straw*. Directed by Shonali Bose, this critically lauded cinematic work delves into the realms of identity, desire, and disability. At its core, the film presents a compelling narrative centering around Laila, a young woman grappling with cerebral palsy, as she embarks on a profound journey of self-discovery. By analyzing the film through the lens of queer and crip theory, this study reveals how the film challenges ableist and heteronormative stereotypes, reclaims disabled and queer bodies from marginalization, and emphasizes the fluidity and complexity of identity. In doing so, the chapter contributes to ongoing discussions on the representation of disabled queer identities in media and culture.

Challenging Stereotypes and Claiming Social Justice

Margarita with a Straw employs various cinematic techniques to subvert the audience's expectations regarding disability and queerness, skillfully challenging stereotypes on multiple levels. The film's use of sound, visual metaphors, and character development serves to destabilize normative depictions of disabled individuals as asexual or desexualized. In one scene, Laila, while seemingly composing lyrics for her college band, listens to explicit audio content and relieves her sexual urges through masturbation. In the aforementioned scene where Laila masturbates, the creative juxtaposition of the rhythmic sound of a train and her sexual pleasure serves as a metaphor for her internal desires breaking free from societal restraints. This audacious moment not only defies the trope of the asexual disabled body but also invites the audience to recognize Laila's complex, layered identity as a sexual being. Through this depiction, the film boldly asserts the presence of sexuality within disabled individuals' lives—an aspect often erased or neglected in mainstream narratives. The film continually subverts audience expectations through its portrayal of Laila's relationships. Laila is not presented as a passive recipient of love or care, a common stereotype associated with disabled individuals. Instead, she is active in her pursuit of romantic and sexual fulfillment, as seen in her bold initiation of a kiss with Dhruv in the Biology lab and later in her complex relationship with Khanum. The film uses intimate close-ups and deliberate pacing during these scenes to emphasize Laila's agency, making it clear that she is not defined by her disability. Her desires and choices are central to her characterization, challenging the trope of disabled people being passive or dependent. Anita Ghai argues that "the assumption that sexuality and disability are mutually exclusive also denies that people with deviant bodies experience sexual desires and refuses them recognition as sexually typical despite their differences" (Ghai 2015, 143). The movie boldly addresses two under-discussed issues within a single narrative: the sexuality of a disabled person and a woman taking the initiative in a sexual encounter. The cinematic portrayal within this film serves as a powerful agent of change in the realm of disability representation, effectively challenging and deconstructing prevailing stereotypes associated with disabled individuals. While a considerable number of novels, plays, short stories, and poems "reinforce oppressive ideas of normalcy, sentimentalise, and solidify stereotypes about disability" (Hall 2016, 4), *Margarita with a Straw* resonates with a positive representation of disability.

The film also subverts audience expectations regarding the caregiver-care receiver dynamic. Traditional media often portrays disabled individuals as burdens on their caregivers. In contrast, *Margarita with a Straw* flips this narrative by showing Laila stepping into the role of caregiver for her mother during her illness. These moments are visually underscored by tender, lingering shots of Laila bathing and massaging her mother, highlighting the emotional and physical labor she performs. This shift in roles invites the audience to rethink preconceived notions about dependence and autonomy in disabled lives. Furthermore, when her father grapples with the emotional turmoil accompanying his wife's battle with cancer, Laila steps in to provide invaluable emotional support, thereby dismantling the stereotype of disabled individuals as mere recipients of care. Khanum, Laila's partner, who is blind, also emerges as a multifaceted character within the narrative. Despite her visual impairment, Khanum actively participates in household chores, skillfully preparing meals, maintaining the cleanliness of their home, and even engaging in public activities and protests. These powerful visuals not only underscore the remarkable capabilities of disabled individuals but also challenge the prevailing misconception that they are burdensome to society.

Moreover, the film's use of public spaces as a backdrop for Laila's experiences also plays a significant role in subverting stereotypes. Laila is frequently depicted navigating bustling, open environments such as college campuses, protests, and city streets, all of which contrast with the conventional image of disabled individuals being confined to private, enclosed spaces. The recurring shots of Laila maneuvering her wheelchair through these dynamic spaces, often without assistance, visually emphasize her independence and agency, subtly challenging the stereotype of disabled people being homebound or socially isolated. She treads public places, to quote Simi Linton, "straightforward, unmasked, and unapologetic" (Linton 1998, 6).

Intriguingly, the film does not restrict its exploration of Laila's identity solely to her disability or sexual orientation. Instead, it presents her as a complex, multi-dimensional character whose identity encompasses her passion for music, her intricate family dynamics, and personal exploration of desires and ambitions. In doing so, the film humanizes queer individuals, reminding viewers that their lives are characterized by richness and diversity that extends far beyond their sexual orientation. Within the context of Laila and Khanum's relationship, the film beautifully emphasizes the depth of their bond, transcending mere sexual fantasies. Through tender moments where they hold hands, the movie portrays a profound, authentic love that serves as a powerful visual symbol, inviting heterosexual viewers to celebrate and recognize the validity of their union. In this way, the film fosters a broader understanding of love and relationships, challenging preconceived notions and encouraging inclusivity. Robert Murphy has rightly commented that "The greatest impediment to a person's taking full part in this society is not his physical flaws, but rather the tissue of myths, fears and misunderstandings that society attaches to them" (Murphy 1990, 113).

By blending these narrative choices with thoughtful cinematic techniques, *Margarita with a Straw* challenges the audience to confront and reevaluate ingrained assumptions about disability and queerness. The film's deliberate, multifaceted representation of Laila's character invites viewers to understand disabled and queer identities as complex, fluid, and fully capable of experiencing and expressing desire, love, and agency.

Intersectionality of Identity and Fluidity

The cinematic narrative deftly navigates the intricate intersectionality of Laila's identity, skillfully illustrating how her lived experience as a queer disabled individual is intricately woven together by the interplay of various facets of her identity. It transcends the boundaries of a single dimension, revealing that her journey transcends the realms of mere disability or sexuality; rather, it offers a profound exploration of the holistic experience of inhabiting the complex space of being both disabled and queer. Moreover, the film serves as a compelling tableau, painting a vivid picture of the rich tapestry of diversity that resides within both the queer and disabled communities. While Laila's experiences remain distinctly her own, they serve as a powerful beacon, illuminating the vast spectrum of narratives and encounters within these communities. Such revelations resonate deeply with the ethos of Queer Crip Studies, which advocates for the recognition of this diversity while honoring the individuality of each person's unique journey.

Laila's decision to terminate her relationship with Dhruv begets a momentous remark from him: "Being friends with normal people won't make you normal" (*Margarita* 2014, 15:41). This utterance, deeply rooted in traditional paradigms, embodies the perspective that often perceives disability as a deviation from societal norms. Michael Warner writes in The Trouble with Normal: Sex, Politics, and the Ethics of Queer Life, "Nearly everyone wants to be normal. And who can blame them, if the alternative is being abnormal, or deviant, or not being one of the rest of us? Put in those terms, there doesn't seem to be a choice at all" (Warner 1999, 53). Dhruv, entrenched in this worldview, subscribes to the notion that disabled individuals are ill-suited for romantic entanglements with their non-disabled counterparts. Consequently, he grapples to reconcile Laila's affection for Nima, the male vocalist of her college band, leading to the dissolution of their romantic connection. This, in turn, propels Laila to embark on a new chapter in her life, departing from her college and enrolling at New York University. During a fervent protest for justice, Laila's path fortuitously crosses with Khanum's, giving birth to a profound friendship. This connection, infused with emotional resonance, serves as the catalyst for the awakening of a previously latent dimension of Laila's sexuality. A pivotal moment unfurls as Khanum's hand gently guides Laila's over a sculpture, evoking an electrifying response within Laila's body. Later, within the hushed confines of a changing room, nestled beside a serene swimming pool, Laila finds herself captivated by Khanum's exposed form, an attraction that crescendos into an impassioned kiss and a subsequent intimate encounter following a night spent at a local pub. Within this newfound relationship, Laila discovers profound contentment. However, a significant turn takes place when, during an interaction with her fellow student, Jared, Laila unexpectedly engages in a moment of physical proximity that transcends the boundaries of friendship. Subsequently, Laila grapples with her inner turmoil and, with a heavy heart, confesses to Khanum the occurrence of this intimate encounter with Jared, which transpired while they were still in a committed relationship. Khanum's reaction to this revelation is charged with complexity; she accuses Laila of seeking to conform to conventional societal norms by embracing heterosexuality as a path towards normalcy. This reaction is emblematic of entrenched societal perceptions that invariably equate heterosexuality with the benchmark of normality. As Farr sarcastically contends, "to do heterosexuality correctly, in other words, is to eradicate deformity" (Farr 2020, 116). In stark contrast, Laila's perspective on her own life experiences is multifaceted and deeply nuanced. As a bisexual individual, she navigates her physical desires with an openness that defies binary categorizations. Simultaneously, she derives profound satisfaction from the validation her disabled body receives when viewed through the lens of the non-disabled male gaze.

Emphasis on Lived Experience

The film masterfully underscores the paramount significance of lived experiences. Laila's narrative doesn't serve as a mere case study, but rather as an intimate odyssey into her innermost desires, her relentless struggles, and her ultimate triumphs. In this cinematic journey, her inner world is vividly brought to life, allowing viewers to forge a profound and emotional connection with her. This emphasis on personal narratives seamlessly aligns with the very essence of both queer and crip studies, dismantling the boundaries that separate us from Laila's profound journey. A genuine narrative plays a crucial role in countering the prevailing collection of biased portrayals of queer and disabled individuals. Siebers argues that "Oppression is driven not by individual, unconscious syndromes but by social ideologies that are embodied, and precisely because ideologies are embodied, their effects are readable, and must be read" (Siebers 2008, 30). Siebers underscores the intricate interconnection between the material, textual, and cultural realms. The cinematic tapestry of *Margarita with a Straw* unfolds against a backdrop that is anything but utopian. The characters that populate this narrative aren't denizens of a fantastical realm; they are beautifully imperfect beings with their own foibles and moments of vulnerability. They unwittingly carry the weight of societal orthodoxies, yet they muster the courage to stand up and protest against the prevailing discourses of the society that seeks to confine them. Sometimes, they emerge victorious, casting aside the shackles that would have otherwise imprisoned their spirits.

From the very outset of the film, a pivotal scene unravels Laila's journey to college, a seemingly ordinary moment that carries profound implications. The

Matador, driven by her mother, becomes a vessel of her aspirations, but it also becomes a stark metaphor for the world she navigates. Upon reaching her destination, Laila emerges as a vivacious individual, her banter with her friend Dhruv brimming with life. Yet, it is in a moment of helplessness, when a non-functioning elevator disrupts her path, that her facial expressions bare her soul. It's here that the absence of a simple ramp underscores society's failure to provide basic accessibility. In a cinematic close-up, Laila's vulnerable expression becomes a poignant reminder of this societal shortcoming, echoing the resounding truth that a person with impairments only becomes disabled when the world fails to accommodate them. In another scene, Laila shares a glimpse of her internal struggles, posting an edited photo on social media. She deliberately conceals her legs and electric wheelchair, a stark reflection of her own discomfort with her body. This act powerfully resonates with the concept of "internalized oppression" (David and Derthick 2014), where marginalized individuals internalize negative societal stereotypes. Her words, when questioned by Khanum about her past dates, speak volumes about her deep-seated fear of rejection: "Why would anyone date me?" (*Margarita* 2014, 47:38), a fear that may have driven her towards a physical union with Jared, despite her commitment to Khanum.

Laila and Khanum's love is a testament to their courage in challenging societal norms. Khanum humorously remarks that no one would even guess that they're lovers, underlining the audacity of their love in the face of societal expectations. Laila's journey takes her to India, where she reveals her bisexuality and love for Khanum to her mother, only to be met with a disparaging "Chii" [Hindi for extreme disgust] (*Margarita* 2014, 1:14:56). Her mother's rejection mirrors the intersection of queerness and disability as being labeled "not normal," a shared struggle that forms a cornerstone of Laila's identity. The accusing of queer/disabled persons as deviant operates to establish heterosexuality and able-bodiedness as dominant discourses in the society. McRuer in his "*Compulsory Able-Bodiedness and Queer/Disabled Existence*" sums up:

> The most successful heterosexual subject is the one whose sexuality is not compromised by disability (metaphorized as queerness); the most successful able-bodied subject is the one whose ability is not compromised by queerness (metaphorized as disability). This consolidation occurs through complex processes of conflation and stereotype: people with disabilities are often understood as somehow queer (as paradoxical stereotypes of the asexual or oversexual person with disabilities would suggest), while queers are often understood as somehow disabled (as an ongoing medicalization of identity, similar to

what people with disabilities more generally encounter, would suggest).
(McRuer 2013, 492-493)

A socio-cultural perspective seeks to prove queer/disabled persons as away
from normalcy to maintain the hegemony of heterosexuality. However, in the
context of the present film, it is in the face of her mother's diagnosis with colon
cancer that acceptance begins to bloom. Khanum, though she ultimately
departs from Laila, offers a glimmer of emotional solace. In the wake of her
mother's passing, Laila embarks on a profound journey of self-discovery,
shedding her old self like a chrysalis. She transforms her appearance, embarks
on a date with herself, and the film culminates in a striking scene. Laila raises a
Margarita cocktail to her own reflection in a vast restaurant mirror, a poignant
toast to her newfound self-acceptance and a vibrant celebration of life's infinite
possibilities.

Limitations and Broadening the Scope Beyond

While *Margarita with a Straw* provides a rich and nuanced exploration of the
intersection of queerness and disability, it is important to recognize the
potential limitations of using a single film as the primary source for analysis.
One limitation lies in the specificity of the film's cultural, geographical, and
narrative context, which may not fully encompass the diverse experiences of
disabled queer individuals across different socio-cultural and political
environments. Laila's story is set within a specific framework—urban India and
New York City—where the availability of resources, opportunities for self-
exploration, and public awareness of disability and queerness might differ
significantly from other global or even regional contexts.

Furthermore, while the film successfully deconstructs certain stereotypes
and introduces complex representations of identity, it remains a singular
narrative that cannot capture the full spectrum of disabled queer experiences.
Every individual's intersectional journey is unique, shaped by factors such as
race, class, gender identity, and socioeconomic status, all of which might
influence how queerness and disability are navigated in daily life. As a result,
relying on *Margarita with a Straw* may inadvertently limit the scope of analysis
by focusing on one representation that might not be entirely reflective of the
multiplicity of disabled queer experiences.

Additionally, cinematic portrayals, while powerful, are inherently shaped by
the vision of the filmmaker and the constraints of the medium. The director's
perspective, along with narrative decisions made for artistic or commercial
purposes, may introduce certain biases or oversimplifications. For instance,
the film prioritizes Laila's sexual awakening and self-discovery, but it may not
engage as deeply with other aspects of queer disabled life, such as systemic

barriers to healthcare, employment, or the day-to-day experiences of navigating inaccessible environments.

That said, the focus on *Margarita with a Straw* offers a compelling entry point for discussions on queer and crip studies, particularly given the film's bold subversion of traditional narratives. However, future research might benefit from comparative analyses of multiple films or forms of media that represent a broader array of disabled queer individuals. Expanding the analysis to include varied cultural representations could provide a more comprehensive understanding of how queerness and disability are depicted in media and how these portrayals shape societal perceptions.

Conclusion

In conclusion, *Margarita with a Straw* serves as a powerful testament to the intricate convergence of queerness and disability, as explored through the lens of queer crip studies. Through its compelling narrative and thought-provoking visuals, the film challenges stereotypes, claims social justice, highlights the intersectionality of identity, and emphasizes the paramount importance of lived experiences. The portrayal of Laila as a complex, multi-dimensional character defies the de-sexualization often associated with disabled individuals, challenging prevailing stereotypes. The film also subverts traditional caregiver dynamics, showcasing the agency and autonomy of disabled individuals, and offers a profound exploration of the holistic experience of being both disabled and queer. Furthermore, the film underscores the significance of personal narratives, allowing viewers to forge a deep emotional connection with Laila's journey. It reminds us that marginalized communities are not utopian ideals but are composed of beautifully imperfect beings who courageously confront societal orthodoxies. The film's exploration of love and relationships fosters a broader understanding of these aspects, challenging preconceived notions and encouraging inclusivity. The intersection of queerness and disability is portrayed as a shared struggle against societal expectations, highlighting the need for acceptance and self-discovery.

In essence, *Margarita with a Straw* exemplifies the potential of cinematic storytelling to break down stereotypes, humanize marginalized communities, and foster a more inclusive and accepting society. It stands as a testament to the richness and diversity of human experiences, irrespective of disability or sexual orientation. As scholars and activists, it is incumbent upon us to recognize and celebrate the profound synergy between queer studies and crip studies, for it has the power to reshape our understanding of identity and liberation, and ultimately contribute to a more just and equitable world for all.

References

Clare, Eli. *Exile and Pride: Disability, Queerness, and Liberation.* Boston: South End Press, 1999.

David, E. J. R., and Annie O. Derthick. "What Is Internalized Oppression, and So What?" In *Internalized Oppression: The Psychology of Marginalized Groups,* edited by E. J. R. David, 1-30. Springer, 2014.

Davis, Lennard J. *Enforcing Normalcy: Disability, Deafness, and the Body.* Verso, 1995.

—. *Bending over Backwards: Disability, Dismodernism, and Other Difficult Positions.* New York University Press, 2002.

Escoffier, Jeffrey and Berubé, Allan. "Queer/Nation." *OUT/LOOK: National Lesbian and Gay Quarterly* 2 (1991):13-14.

Farr, Jason S. "Crip Gothic: Affiliations of Disability and Queerness in Horace Walpole's The Castle of Otranto (1764). In *The Routledge Companion to Literature and Disability,* edited by Alice Hall, 109-119. Routledge, 2020.

Garland-Thomson, Rosemarie. *Extraordinary Bodies: Figuring Physical Disability in American Culture and Literature.* Columbia University Press, 1997.

Ghai, Anita. *Rethinking Disability in India.* Routledge, 2015.

Hall, Alice. *Literature and Disability.* Routledge, 2016. https://doi.org/10.4324/9781315726595

Linton, Simi. *Claiming Disability: Knowledge and Identity.* New York University Press, 1998.

Margarita with a Straw. Directed by Shonali Bose, Viacom 18, 2015. Netflix.

McRuer, Robert. "The World-Making Potential of Contemporary Crip/Queer Literary and Cultural Production." In *The Cambridge Companion to Literature and Disability,* edited by Clare Barker and Stuart Murray, 139-154. Cambridge University Press, 2017.

—."Compulsory Able-Bodiedness and Queer/Disabled Existence." In *The Routledge Queer Studies Reader,* edited by Donald E. Hall et al., 488-497. Routledge, 2013.

Murphy, Robert. *The Body Silent.* Norton, 1990.

Sedgwick, Eve Kosofsky. "Queer and Now." In *Tendencies,* edited by Michéle Aina Barale et al., 1-22. Duke University Press, 1983.

Siebers, Tobian. *Disability Theory.* The University of Michigan Press, 2008. https://doi.org/10.3998/mpub.309723

Warner, Michael. *The Trouble with Normal: Sex, Politics, and the Ethics of Queer Life.* The Free Press, 1999.

Chapter Four

Shahria Sharmin's *Call Me Heena*: Decolonial Heterotopic Space of the Photograph and Representation of the Hijra

Iraboty Kazi
University of Western Ontario

Abstract

This paper explores the heterotopia and the queering of space in relation to the hijra family and identity. The term hijra, which has no exact match in the Western taxonomy of gender, is used in South Asia to define those biologically designated as male or intersex at birth with female gender identity. Hijras live on the margins of society where they are both hypervisible as an *other* and invisible in matters of political representation, legal protection, and education. Although hijras have captured the interest of photographers since early colonial photography, recent works by South Asian female artists shift the focus from simply displaying their bodies to attempting to share the hijra subjectivity. Bangladeshi photographer Shahria Sharmin's ethereal black and white series, *Call Me Heena* (2012-), presents the hijras in their private spaces. I argue that the space presented in the photographs is heterotopic, seemingly existing outside of identifiable time or space, thus allowing self-expression when it is not otherwise possible. The hijras in the photographs often seek traditional roles of mother and/or lover, which is considered taboo in South Asian society because of their gender identity. The heterotopic space of the photograph allows for the exploration of the hijras' desires in ways that subvert gender norms while still preserving traditional ideas of the family. Thus, the heterotopic space allows enough distance from reality to explore fantasies while still being rooted in reality.

Keywords: Heterotopic Space, Photography, Hijra Representations.

***

*Photographs are painful, not only in their content sometimes … but
sometimes their truth-telling, their performance of histories, their
reality has a painfulness – rawness…They were intended to present some
closure within a specific [colonial] body of practice, but they present
instead, points of fracture, an opening out. Through the photograph's
points of fracture, the rawness, we can begin to register the possibility of
a history that is no longer founded on traditional models of experience
and reference* (Edwards 2010, 6).

The term hijra, which has no exact match in the Western taxonomy of gender,
is used in South Asia to define those biologically designated as male or intersex
at birth with a feminine gender identity who eventually adopt feminine gender
roles (Sharmin 2020). Although they can fall under the umbrella of
transgenderism, they are often mislabeled as hermaphrodites, eunuchs, or
transsexual women (Sharmin 2020). The current politically agreed-upon term for
the hijra is the third gender. Hijra communities face extreme marginalization as
they are excluded from almost all aspects of society. Although hijras have
captured the interest (and imagination) of photographers since the early days
of colonial photography, a limited number of projects, such as Dhaka-based
freelance photographer Shahria Sharmin's *Call Me Heena* (2012-), attempt to
portray the hijra from a subjective perspective. The portraits in Sharmin's series
challenge broader social stigma and ignorance towards this misunderstood
community by providing an intimate view of the hijra. Sharmin embarked on
the project in 2012 after meeting and forming bonds with a hijra community,
which allowed her to photograph them as they travelled from Bangladesh to
India with hopes of finding more acceptance. Sharmin has since displayed the
series in numerous international exhibitions and online and has received
numerous awards, positive reviews from LGBTQIA+ organizations, and
attention from Bangladeshi and international press. Sharmin has received
several prizes, including the Magnum Photography Awards (2017), the Pride
Photo Award's Getting Closer category (2014), and second place winner of the
Alexia Foundation student grant (2014). The series was selected in FotoVisura
Spotlight Exhibition (Brisbane), the Internazionale d'Arte LGBTE (Turin), the
Lightseekers & Asian Women Photographers' Showcase (Leicester), the
Obscura Festival (Penang), the Photissima Art Fair (Torino), Pride Photo Award
exhibition (Amsterdam) and Open Society Foundations, and Moving Walls 23
group exhibition. In the essay, I will argue that the intimate portraits are an
attempt to decolonize the portrayal of hijras, as these images show a shift from
the ethnographic (colonial) eye to a focus on their subjectivity.

Although British rule of India ended in 1947, the coloniality of power that
remains affects the way the hijras are represented in mainstream society. As
Walter D. Mignolo explains, the double process indicated by Quijano is the

inscription of the colonial difference and the consequence of the coloniality of power (Mignolo 2002, 82). Decoloniality, as explained by Catherine Walsh, "seeks to make visible, open up, and advance radically distinct perspectives and positionalities that displace Western rationality as the only framework and possibility of existence, analysis and thought" (Walsh 2020, 17). The black and white space presented in the photographs is a heterotopic space, which seems to exist outside of any identifiable time or space to allow self-expression when it is not otherwise possible. In his short 1967 lecture, "*Des Espaces Autres*" ("Of Other Spaces"), Foucault describes the heterotopia as "an effectively enacted utopia in which the real sites, all the other real sites that can be found within the culture, are simultaneously represented, contested, and inverted" (Foucault 1984, 3). He names several "counter sites," such as cemeteries, brothels, holidays, and prisons, which are outside of the ordinary and disrupt time and space. While the hijra communities and their unique set of rituals and social structures can be considered heterotopic, the photographic space is a counter-space that differs from mainstream society and the sites where the hijras inhabit. In the heterotopic space of the photographs, the hijras are presented as subjects with voices. Through the simple, dark background reminiscent of a studio, she de-emphasizes the external elements and dislocates the hijra from the colonial structure of the photograph and reality, instead creating room for their social structures, practices, and desires to shine.

Brief Overview of the Hijra Community in Bangladesh

The hijra community has a place in South Asian society that is "both culturally and historically accepted; whilst at the same time being a discriminated minority outside of most functions within the society" (Stenqvist 2015, 8). Although hijras are a visible social group, large pockets of hijra culture are unclear to most South Asians. It should be noted that recent "scholarship has added considerably to our understanding of hijra, and has complicated over-romanticized representations of the hijra, highlighting the myriad modalities of differentiation, including locality, kinship, globalization, religion, language, gender and class, through which hijra subjectivities are produced and inflected" (Cohen 1995; Agrawal 1997; Reddy 2005; Hall 1997; Nanda 1999). Nonetheless, contemporary representations of the hijra may be seen as a continuation of a longstanding colonial attempt to contain their apparent unintelligibility (Gannon 2009). In the heteronormative religious South Asian societies, the hijra's presence represents a devaluing of gender binaries and the stability of genders (Butler 1988, 520). The subversion of gender norms and movement between the genders historically led to the hijras being viewed as semi-divine beings with the power to curse people in Hinduism and as powerful intercessors of Muslim Mughal emperors. "Hijras have been part of South Asia's culture for thousands of years but it was only when the British came to power in India in 1897 that outraged colonists introduced a law classing them as criminals" (Mullin 2014). Adnan Hossain explains: "[T]he apparent recalcitrance and irreducibility of hijra to any neat conceptual category not only troubled the British colonial mind but also posed a direct challenge to the classificatory imperatives of the colonial administration" (Hossain 2012, 496). Living in a "simultaneously mythic and real" space outside of the norm, the small community that earned money dancing was seen as a threat to the public's moral and, more importantly, colonial authority (Foucault 1986, 4). In *Governing Gender and Sexuality in Colonial India,* Jennifer Hinchy explains that British officials began considering them "ungovernable," saying that they evoked images of "filth, disease, contagion and contamination" (Biswas 2019). Thus, the British launched a campaign to reduce the number of eunuchs and hijras with the objective of causing their extinction (Biswas 2019). Connected to the British legislative treatment of hijra, British photographers sought to capture the hijras as subjects of Western interest, in essence, representative of difference and Indian exoticism. Early colonial photographs of hijras, such as *Gurmah, Khunsa, or Hijra, reputed hermaphrodite, Eastern Bengal,* c. 1860s, were taken mostly by British commercial photographers and often used for collections of racial and caste types. The hijras in these types of photographs are seen more as curiosities rather than humans with thoughts. Although the hijras resisted and survived colonial attempts to exterminate them, the impact of colonial laws led them to be socially excluded and financially ruined. To this day, the colonial treatment of the hijras continues to shape people's perceptions of them, as Hinchy states, "ungovernable people due to their social marginality, perceived criminality, sexuality and the various ways that they affront notions of respectability" (Hinchy 2019, 256).

Social and familial ostracization leads most hijras to leave their homes to live in communities where they feel a strong sense of belonging. These groups give them the shelter of a family and the warmth of human relationships. Hijra communities are matriarchal hierarchies with the *chelas* (subordinates) giving half of their earnings to the *gurus* (leaders) who protect them from the police and others when they are harassed or arrested on prostitution charges. They traditionally earned their living by singing and dancing during weddings and after births, which is based on the cultural belief that hijras can bless one's house with prosperity and fertility (Sharmin 2020). Due to the decline of that tradition, hijras make a living by collecting money from shopkeepers (using profanities and yelling at shopkeepers until they receive money to leave), begging, or prostitution. As Sharmin states: "They do not have any school to study, no temple to pray in, no government and private organizations would want to see them in their employee list. They have no access to the legal system nor do even health service providers welcome them" (Sharmin 2020). Despite being one of the most marginalized groups in Bangladesh, the hijras' efforts for legal rights led the Bangladeshi government to recognize hijras as belonging to a third gender in November 2013. This legal recognition allows them to have IDs, passports, entry into educational institutions, and the right to vote. This promising move, however, was undermined by the fact that "Bangladesh does not have a policy outlining the measures individuals must take to legally change the gender marker on their official documents from 'male' to 'hijra,' and there is no clarity about who qualifies as a hijra." For example, in January 2015, the health ministry issued a memorandum requesting that "necessary steps are taken to identify authentic hijras by conducting a thorough medical check-up" (Knight 2019, 2). However, "during these so-called "examinations," physicians ordered non-medical hospital staff such as custodians to touch the hijras' genitals while groups of staff and other patients observed and jeered— sometimes in private rooms, sometimes in public spaces" (Knight 2019, 2). Thus, this formal designation does little to improve the everyday realities of being excluded by society, as few are able to get legal protection or representation.

Sharmin's History with the Hijra Community

Figure 4.1: Shahria Sharmin, At dawn Nayan (24) goes to work at a garments factory and earns what's perceived as honest income by her family. But at dusk, she returns to her community, *Call Me Heena*, 2012.

The project builds on Shahria Sharmin's interest in photography's connection to identity, exploring and expressing the diversity of human experiences. As she states, "*Call Me Heena* is my attempt to show the beauty in Hijra lives, despite the challenges and discrimination they face" (Sharmin 2020). Her desire to 'show the beauty' is immediately evident through the aesthetically beautiful portraits of hijras alone or as duos. However, the images and captions do not hide or aestheticize their pain; instead, pain, both physical and emotional, is depicted alongside their stories of kinship, love, and dreams. In the photographs taken by a wooden instant camera, the play of light and shadow creates an ambiance of darkness and intimacy. These spaces show the hijra subjects and their individual experiences on a personal level. Without evidence of the heavy, colorful make-up that is typically associated with the hijras or the social stigma towards them, Sharmin seems to highlight their experiences as humans. The desire to challenge the social stigmas towards the hijra is reflective of Sharmin's own journey of changing her perceptions towards the marginalized group. Typical of many Bangladeshis, Sharmin grew up believing that hijras were "less than human" as "their physical appearance, their behaviour and their general way of life," she explains, "set them apart in her country's conservative society" (Brooks 2017). She met Nayan [Figure 4.1], one of the five hijra workers among a workforce of four thousand, when she visited the factory with a plan to create a photo essay about laborers working in Bangladesh's garment industry for a school project. Sharmin's relationship with the hijras, particularly the then fifty-one-year-old Heena, led her to abandon the garments factory story for an initially self-financed series. Sharmin says of Heena: "She made me see how wrong I was … She opened her life to me, made me a part of her world and helped me to see beyond the word Hijra. She made me understand her, and others who live in her community, as the mothers, daughters, friends and lovers that they actually are" (Sharmin 2017). Sharmin photographs Hijra women in diverse circumstances. For example, some are garment workers, while others make ends meet through prostitution; some openly identify as hijra, while others have not come out to their families (Kail 2014).

In her own words, Sharmin's series "aims to challenge the persisting social stigmas attached to the Hijras community by releasing images that the artist believes convey a different reality to the world" (Brooks 2014). While the photograph always includes the photographer's point of view as the person behind the lens, in Sharmin's case, she does not attempt to present herself as the authority of the narrative. Instead, she takes a denarrativized, multi-perspective approach as she states: "There are many perspectives to each story, and… photography should illuminate a story, not define it" (Brooks 2014). Her experience as someone outside of the hijra community who formed relationships with them allows her to be a witness. Her approach to photographing her subject includes:

> spending hours with them without taking a single photo, often having conversations over meals about various issues. This time is vital for building trust and making collaborative artistic decisions with her subjects. Usually Sharmin talks with them "about the photograph I want to take." After that, she said, her subjects "give me some ideas or guidelines on how they would like to be represented. I haven't noticed much anxiety among them about the way of their representation, rather I found them quite confident on what they are looking for, and normally I do not deviate from their intentions. (Sharmin 2017)

Sharmin's closeness to her subjects challenges the ethnographical norm of the detached photographer. The detached viewpoint advocated by early European photographers, such as Samuel Bourne (1834–1912), helps maintain the idea of the "unbiased" indexicality of the ethnographic photograph. However, Sharmin, like contemporary South Asian postcolonial photographers, does not try to capture the body of the hijra in her image. Instead, she collaborates with them to best represent them. While the camera will always include the photographer's input as the person behind the lens, in the case of Sharmin, it is not the sole voice of authority, as her subjects have agency. Furthermore, the shift from the detachment between the subject and the photographer is presented not only in the photograph but also beyond the event of the photograph. Sharmin, as a mother of two daughters, is interested in the dynamics between her subjects and their families—both their birth families and their chosen ones. Although many of her subjects yearn to return to their biological families, they are often unable to do so because their relatives, especially their fathers, do not accept them (Sharmin 2017). Similar to Indian photographers Tejal Shah and Dayanita Singh, who have photographed and built relationships with hijras, Sharmin does not present herself as a seemingly invisible presence trying to capture the hijras' struggles to expose them to the world for profit. Instead, these artists aim to bring change beyond the act of taking the photograph. For example, Singh met Mona Ahmed, a hijra, on an assignment that led to a decades-long friendship until Mona's death in 2017. Their friendship was documented in Singh's collection of photographs and letters in the 2001 book, *Myself Mona Ahmed*. Similarly, the latter part of Sharmin's project shows portraits of her hijra friends with their families, hoping to spur reconciliation on a personal level (Blaustein 2015). The colonial detachment between the photographer and the photographed subject is replaced with invested interest and allyship.

An interesting aspect of the series is Sharmin's choice to use short captions or quotes from the photographed subject rather than titles. While inscriptions are a common practice, Sharmin's are based on conversations between her and the subjects. During the process, she records quotes from her subjects that reflect the complexity of their experiences (Blaustein 2015). She subverts the colonial authority of the photographer as the subjects' voices are shared along with their bodies. Sharmin states: "Through my work, I am hoping to give a voice to the voiceless. Photography has always been an extremely effective tool to challenge the social stigma and help unleash a different reality to the world" (Sharmin 2020). Akin to Singh's *Myself Mona Ahmed*, we are made aware from the title that the project attempts to present the hijra's point of view as it says, "call me Heena" and not "call her Heena." Although framed within the structure of Sharmin's style of photography and writing of the caption, the subjectivity of the sitters is brought to the forefront. This is highlighted by how much and what kind of information is shared with the viewer. Contemporary ethnographic photographers of the hijra either write over-generalized statements, such as "They often wear decorative, thick make up" by Danish photographer Jan Moeller Hansen or overly detailed descriptions of sexual abuse, marginalization, and hardship. For example, Dutch photographer Peter Bos' untitled photograph shows a young smiling hijra posing among trees, but the seemingly serene image is contrasted with the painful inscription: "Phanita is 35 years old and from her 20th hijra. Phanita has its permanent place at the intersection in Kolkata. She doesn't beg, but offers herself for sex. The sexual acts take place in the bushes just next to the road in the park. She is not yet 'helped', and now she is saving for surgery to have her penis removed…The costs are approximately 40000 rupees (€520)" (Bos 2019). Unlike his other photographs of the hijras (such as the photograph of the guru, Deepti "proudly" showing her lack of a penis), Phanita's image may not fully expose the hijra's body but the description does. He exposes intimate details about her private parts to a Western audience that one normally would not be comfortable publicly disclosing. His catering to a European audience is reinforced by the conversion of the Indian Rupees to Euros. Sharmin's captions, on the other hand, do not share the typical narrative of sexual and physical abuse in an expository manner. Instead, they seem to follow the social protocols of the conservative Bangladeshi society since conversations between most Bangladeshis would not include the things mentioned by Bos. Just like her photographs, when reading Sharmin's captions, the viewers are not privy to all their secrets. Sharmin's photographs provide an introduction to further communication and discoveries, which will be based on the hijra subject's willingness to share. Sharmin may be using her position as an 'average' (heterosexual Cis-gendered) Bangladeshi woman to act as an intercessor figure between the hijra and the audience. Hijras often use sexual lingo as a defense mechanism or to make money from shop owners paying them to stop verbally harassing them. The quotes Sharmin uses do not include any overtly sexual terms, thus presenting the hijra in a way that she might deem to be favorable. While this leads to the hijra being presented within a framework, it allows viewers to hear the hijra in a way that is different from how they are normally perceived. Furthermore, based on the numerous ethnographic studies and media coverage of the hijras, it is apparent that there is at least some awareness among South Asians of the hijras' marginalization. Thus, photographs that use shock as a call for action may not be as effective if people are already somewhat aware of the situation. The hijras' differences lead them to be pitied as outsiders rather than viewed as members of our society. The captions, which are phrased in a way that gives glimpses into the hijra subjectivity, encourage them to be seen not as suffering *other* but as fellow humans with agency.

Displacement from Time and Space

Figure 4.2: Shahria Sharmin, "I like to see guys get attracted to me, like other women"- Jesmin, 24, *Call Me Heena*, 2012.

Sharmin's series follows a lineage of photographing marginalized transgender communities to give them a place in cultural memories, as they are often excluded from history. Interestingly, her images do not have any geographical markers to identify their locations despite Sharmin following the hijras' journey from Bangladesh to India. Sharmin followed the hijras' journey from Bangladesh to India. This contrasts what scholar Eduardo Cadava terms "photographic self-archiving," which "positions bodies within specific chronotopes - it matters to some people when you went to France that the trace of the Eiffel Tower in the distance is the one in the center of Paris and not a simulacrum: as Bourdieu says, it 'consecrates the unique encounter'" (Pinney 2014, 459). Sharmin's photographs, which appear to be shot in rooms or other unidentifiable spaces, challenge the positioning of the hijras within recognizable chronotopes. I argue that the lack of identifiable locations makes the spaces heterotopic (Foucault 1986, 4). Their blankness allows for the contestation of space and the creation of alternative spaces. While Sharmin's photographs are taken in the real site, the space in the images blurs the reality of the space. Interestingly, even in the rare images that include a crowd, the outside world is in the shadows. Nothing visible indicates any change or movement; instead, most of her photographs appear to be shot in rooms or other unidentifiable spaces. Foucault states: "Places of this kind are outside of all places, even though it may be possible to indicate their location in reality" (Foucault 1986, 4). In Sharmin's works, such as *"I like to see guys get attracted to me, like other women"- Jesmin, 24* [Figure 4.2], there is a spotlight that seems to be shining on Jesmin to render her visible to the audience, yet Jesmin's side-profile face and upper body are barely visible in the dark photograph. Based on the presence of the light, it is likely that she is on stage, yet there is no indication of the location, audience size, or her role. The people's faces are hidden from our view, thus making it difficult to connect Jesmin's presence to the outside world and the people's reactions to the hijra. It shows the presence of an audience, yet they, like the rest of the outside world, are in the shadows.

In *"Notes from the Surface of the Image: Photography, Postcolonialism, and Vernacular Modernism,"* Christopher Pinney explains how postcolonial photography eschews colonial strategies of depth and indexicality through a widely dispersed "vernacular modernism" that allow the possibilities for cultural reinvention" (Pinney 2014, 451). In these practices, the surface becomes a site of the refusal of the depth that characterized colonial representational regimes, which "positioned people and objects deep within chronotopic certainties as they sought stable identities in places from which they could not escape" (Pinney 2014, 450). Postcolonial practices negate the concern with fixing bodies in particular times and places by treating the body as a surface that is completely mutable and mobile, capable of being situated anywhere (Pinney 2014, 459). In Pinney's example of the studios in Nagda, India, the city's people reject being photographed in the actual space of Nagda in favor of the diverse backdrops found within the photographer's studio (Pinney 2014, 459). Akin to the use of different backdrops, Sharmin's series shows fractures in place and time using dark backgrounds. The dark atmospheric space makes it seem as if the photographs were taken in the dark, but it is impossible to tell when the photographs were taken. As Foucault writes, heterotopias not only have a spatial dimension but are "linked to slices in time—which is to say that they open onto what might be termed, for the sake of symmetry, heterochronies" (Foucault 1986, 4). There is a sense of temporal dislocation as the images seem to exist outside the boundaries of time, thus challenging the practices of either excluding them or placing the hijra within the structure of the chronicles and archives of history. Furthermore, the photographs show the type of spaces, such as an alley, room, or water, the subject is in, without giving an indication of the actual location. This erasure of the location takes away the practice of situating the hijra in their "places" – both physically and socially. Thus, as Cadava says, "[p]hotograph can be used to position bodies and faces within history, and it can also be used as a means of escape" (Pinney 2014, 459).

"Backgrounds do not simply substitute the absence of their referents, but also create a space for exploration" (Pinney 2014, 460). In the case of the Nagda studios, this exploration is often geographic, as one can travel from Goa to Mandu to Agra merely by standing in front of different walls. According to Pinney, studios also function as "chambers of dreams where personal explorations of an infinite range of alteregos is possible" through the adoption of gestures and through the deployment of costumes and props (Pinney 2014, 461). Thus, in this case, photography is prized not for its ability to produce indexical traces, but rather as a creative transformative space of the image that allows its subject to "come out better" (Pinney 2014, 461) The use of alter egos can be considered the basis of queer Indian photographer, Tejal Shah's *Hijra Fantasy Series* (2006), part of the multi-media exhibition *What Are You?* (2006). Shah creates lavish, multi-layered studio portraits of hijra referencing well-known literary (*The barge she sat in, like a burnished throne/burned on the water*), cinematic (*Southern Siren—Maheshwari*), and religious traditions (*You Too Can Touch the Moon - Yashoda with Krishna*). In the space of the studio and the photograph, the hijras are displaced from reality and transformed into glamorous versions of their dreams. For example, *The barge she sat in, like a burnished throne/burned on the water* depicts well-known hijra rights activist and actress Laxmi Narayan Tripathi as a contemporary, queer and Indian version of Cleopatra based on conversations about Tripathi's obsession with the historical figure (Shah 2020).

Figure 4.3: Shahria Sharmin, Always desiring to be a mother I have adopted Boishakhi. But I wonder what if she calls me father someday! Salma (27), *Call Me Heena*, 2012.

Rather than exploring alter egos such as a poet or film star in the Nagda studios or Shah's pieces, the hijras in Sharmin's photographs explore their desires to be a mother, lover, or desire for kinship. The ethereal photographs become grounds for exploring their fantasies while contemplating the complexities of their reality. In *Always desiring to be a mother I have adopted Boishakhi. But I wonder what if she calls me father someday! Salma (27)* [Figure 4.3], the audience sees what appears to be an ordinary image of a loving mother lying on a bed, caressing her baby. Along with the bed, the dresser behind the pair indicates that this may be a bedroom. The intimacy of the private space is reinforced by the closed door. The nearly naked baby, which is common in hot weather in tropical Bangladesh, connotes a sense of warmth, both physical and emotional. Aside from the unusual placement of a dove, which is a recurring symbol of freedom that appears throughout the series, the audience is presented with an ordinary yet poignant image of a loving mother gazing into her child's eyes. What makes this common image of mother and child subversive is the gender identity of the hijra. What is considered fantasy for the hijra is part of everyday life for non-hijra people. The photographic space that allows for an exploration of these fantasies also brings forth the real issues and fears, such as Salma's worry about being addressed as "father" by an older Boishakhi. In this space, we see the hijra as a mother, but her worries remind us of the outside world, where her physical body is given precedence over gender identity and desires. The fear may relate to other issues sometimes faced by the hijra who adopt children, one of which is the potential of the authorities or even a guru to take the child away from the hijra mother. This was famously the case with an Indian hijra, Mona Ahmed. Thus, the heterotopic space of the photograph allows for a distancing from reality through the exploration of fantasies, but distancing allows for space to acknowledge real issues.

Figure 4.4: Shahria Sharmin, Aporupa, 27, used to sell eggs. Now she sells her body dwelling under a Guru with ten others in a small room, *Call Me Heena*, 2012.

As mentioned, Sharmin's photographs do not aim to "capture" the hijras for documentary purposes, instead, she hopes that her "work will help the Hijras to find a breathing space in a claustrophobic society like ours and it will help them to find new friends in their friendless world" (Brooks 2014). The "breathing space" of the photographs is outside of heteronormative spaces, thus allowing the hijra to present themselves without judgment. *Aporupa, 27, used to sell eggs. Now she sells her body dwelling under a Guru with ten others in a small room* [Figure 4.4] depicts a corner of a room where two hijras appear to be in the process of getting ready. A shirtless Aporupa is shown sitting on a bed holding a small mirror or compact in one hand while applying eye makeup with the other. The camera focuses on Aporupa while the unnamed, out-of-focus hijra in the foreground looks away from the camera. In the heterotopic space, the hijra is not depicted as an 'other'; instead, their practices are presented as part of everyday life. In mainstream South Asian society, someone in a biologically male body applying make-up would be abhorrent, but in the space of Sharmin's photograph, seeing Aporupa doing so does not appear shocking. Aporupa is topless, which highlights her biologically male body, yet her familiar concentrated process of makeup application shifts the attention to what is deemed traditionally feminine. This mixture of masculine and feminine, which complicates the gender binaries, leads to societal misunderstanding of the hijras. This is also emphasized in the caption for her photograph of Heena, *"I feel like a mermaid. My body tells me that I am a man but my soul tells me that I am a woman. I am like a flower, a flower that is made of paper. I shall always be loved from a distance, never to be touched and no smell to fall in love with." Heena, 51,* In this space of the photograph, the mixing of genders is not questioned; instead, gender is deconstructed, thus allowing the viewer to hopefully rethink binaries. Sharmin challenges the persisting social stigmas attached to the hijras by conveying a different reality to the audience.

Light and Shadow as Veils

Figure 4.5: Shahria Sharmin, Nishi, 21, waiting for the man of her dreams, *Call Me Heena*, 2012.

Figure 4.6: Shahria Sharmin, Riya's (29) daily afternoon conversations with death. Cancer for now has charged one leg, the rest will go through an unknown count of days to the end. The Hijra community has no use for Riya, she has returned from Delhi to her birth givers to end slowly, *Call Me Heena*, 2012.

The dark atmospheric spaces and shadows in Sharmin's photographs obscure parts of the images, thus limiting what is available for the viewer's gaze. The literal veils, in images such *Nishi (21) is waiting for the man of her dream* [Figure 4.5] and *Riya's (29) daily afternoon conversations with death. Cancer for now has charged one leg, the rest will go through an unknown count of days to the end. The Hijra community has no use for Riya, she has returned from Delhi to her birth givers to end slowly* [Figure 4.6], hide parts or the entirety of the subjects' faces. In the photograph of Nishi, the lone subject looks directly at the camera behind a diaphanous patterned fabric (presumably, a *saree* or a *dupatta*) that obscures part of her face and chest. Due to the placement of the lighting, a shadow of the outline of her head is cast on the veil, further obscuring the view of Nishi's face. At the same time, the patterned fabric highlights the hijra's femininity, as wearing women's clothes is closely tied to the hijra's identity. She seems to be both inviting and distancing herself from the viewers' gaze. Societal views towards hijras are contradictory, as they are considered by most to be distasteful yet also seen as being mythologically related to fertility. Most Bangladeshis would not want to be seen interacting with them, yet the rate of hijra prostitution is rising. What is lost in the contradictions is the nuances of Nishi's (and others like her) very human desires, some of which are mentioned in the captions.

In the similarly veiled photograph of Riya, the caption and image replace dreams with a more tragic story of illness and impending death. Since Sharmin does not provide information about her artistic decisions, I am assuming, based on her relationship with the hijras, that Riya may have chosen not to show her face. The veil allows Nishi and Riya the agency to choose privacy from the gaze of the viewer. Like other heterotopic sites, the space in the photographs appears accessible, yet not everything is allowed to be seen. "Everyone can enter into the heterotopic sites, but in fact, that is only an illusion—we think we enter where we are, by the very fact that we enter, excluded" (Foucault 1986, 8). In *The Colonial Harem*, the Algerian poet Malek Alloula analyzed the role of photography as "the fertilizer of the colonial vision [producing] stereotypes in the manner of great seabirds producing guano" (Alloula 1986, 4). The veil that Algerian women presented to the colonial vision was received as an affront by photographers ("the whiteness of the veil becomes the symbolic equivalent of blindness: a leukoma, a white speck on the eye of the photographer and his viewpoint"), and a vengeance of visibility and nudity was wreaked on this inviolability that so deeply "haunt[ed] the photographer-voyeur" (Alloula 1986, 4). Using this theory, Sharmin's postcolonial photograph sees the veil not as a threat but as a form of protection from the colonial eye. The photographer is not haunted by the 'inviolability' but supports it, thus reshaping the relationship between the "photographer-voyeur" and the subject. The veil both acts as a means of sexual expression and also as a "symbolic equivalent of blindness" for the viewer that they do not want to expose.

Conclusion

In contrast to the studies on the social conditions and exclusions of the hijras, research on artistic works representing hijras is still limited. While ethnographic studies from Adnan Hossain, Tahmina Hal, and others are extremely helpful in conveying hijra culture and marginalization, they discuss the hijra as a group and do not provide insight into the hijra subjectivity. Sharmin's series does not portray a generalized study of the hijras; instead, she presents individual stories portraying the experiences of those struggling against the world just to live as their true selves. Sharmin stated: "I hope my work will help amplify Hijra voices and inspire Hijras to open even more space for themselves within Bangladeshi society." The photographs show the agency of the hijras despite the horrible conditions they face. Although social change is slow to happen, these works provide a glimmer of hope for more acceptance as Sharmin herself changed her own views on the hijras.

Bibliography

Alloula, Malek. *The Colonial Harem*. Minneapolis: University of Minnesota Press, 1986. https://doi.org/10.5749/j.ctttth83

Biswas, Soutik. "How Britain Tried to 'Erase' India's Third Gender." *BBC News* (London), May 31, 2019. https://www.bbc.com/news/world-asia-india-48442934

Blaustein, Jonathan. "Bangladesh's Third Gender." *The New York Times* (New York), March 18, 2015. https://lens.blogs.nytimes.com/2015/03/18/bangladeshs-third-gender/

Bos, Peter. "HIJRA." Peter Bos Photography Eindhoven, The Netherlands, 2019. https://www.studiopeterbos.com/hijra/

Brooks, Katherine. "Spectacular Black-And-White Portraits Shed Light in Bangladesh's Third Gender." *HuffPost Canada* (Toronto), December 7, 2017. https://www.huffingtonpost.ca/entry/hijras_n_5839324?ri18n=true

Butler, Judith. "Performative Acts and Gender Constitution: An Essay in Phenomenology and Feminist Theory." *Theatre Journal* 40, no. 4 (1988): 519–531. https://doi.org/10.2307/3207893

Das, Rajorshi. "Representation and Categorization: Understanding the Hijra and Transgender Identities through Personal Narratives." *Rupkatha Journal on Interdisciplinary Studies in Humanities* 7, no. 3 (September 1, 2015): 196–205.

Edwards, Elizabeth. *Raw Histories: Photographs, Anthropology and Museums*. Oxford: Berg Publishers, 2010.

Foucault, Michel. "Of Other Spaces: Utopias and Heterotopias." Translated by Jay Miskowiec. *Architecture /Mouvement/ Continuité* (October 1984): 1–9.

Hinchy, Jessica. *Governing Gender and Sexuality in Colonial India: The Hijra, c.1850-1900*. Cambridge: Cambridge University Press, 2019.

Hossain, Adnan. "Beyond Emasculation: Being Muslim and Becoming Hijra in South Asia." *Asian Studies Review* 36, no. 4 (December 1, 2012): 495–513. https://doi.org/10.1080/10357823.2012.739994

--- "The Paradox of Recognition: Hijra, Third Gender and Sexual Rights in Bangladesh." *Culture, Health & Sexuality* 19, no. 12 (December 2, 2017): 1418–1431. https://doi.org/10.1080/13691058.2017.1317831

Jebin, Lubna, and Umme Farhana. "The Rights of Hijra in Bangladesh: An Overview." *Journal of Nazrul University* 3, no. 1 & 2 (2015): 1–10.

Kail, Ellyn. "Dreamy Portraits Capture Hijra, Bangladesh's 'Third Gender'." Feature Shoot, December 5, 2014. https://www.featureshoot.com/2014/09/dreamy-portraits-capture-hijra-bangladeshs-third-gender/

Khan, Sharful Islam et al. "Living on the Extreme Margin: Social Exclusion of the Transgender Population (Hijra) in Bangladesh." *Journal of Health, Population and Nutrition* 27, no. 4 (August 1, 2009): 441–51.

Killen, Gemma. "Archiving the Other or Reading Online Photography as Queer Ephemera." *Australian Feminist Studies* 32, no. 91-92 (April 3, 2017): 58–74. https://doi.org/10.1080/08164649.2017.1357005

Knight, Kyle. "'I Want to Live with My Head Held High': Abuses in Bangladesh's Legal Recognition of Hijras." Human Rights Watch, June 6, 2017. https://www.

hrw.org/report/2016/12/23/i-want-live-my-head-held-high/abuses-bangla
deshs-legal-recognition-hijras.

Mignolo, Walter D. "The Geopolitics of Knowledge and the Colonial Difference."
South Atlantic   Quarterly 101 (1) (2000): 57–96. https://doi.org/10.1215/0038
2876-101-1-57

Mullin, Gemma. "Poignant Pictures Which Show Life for the Outcast
Transgender People in Bangladesh." *Daily Mail Online* (London), September
24, 2014. https://www.dailymail.co.uk/news/article-2767125/Poignant-pictures
-life-outcast-transgender-people-Bangladesh.html.

Pinney, Christopher. "Chapter 16. Notes from the Surface of the Image:
Photography, Postcolonialism, and Vernacular Modernism." In *Empires of
Vision: A Reader* edited by Martin Jay and Sumathi Ramaswamy, 450-470.
New York: Duke University Press, 2014.

Reddy, Gayatri. *With Respect to Sex: Negotiating Hijra Identity in South India.*
New Delhi: Yoda Press, 2006. https://doi.org/10.1055/s-2006-956452

Shah, Tejal. "Tejal Shah." Brooklyn Museum: Tejal Shah. Accessed March 26,
2020.https://www.brooklynmuseum.org/eascfa/about/feminist_art_base/t
ejal-shah.

Shahria, Sharmin. "Call Me Heena." PhMuseum. Accessed October 12, 2020.
https://phmuseum.com/projects/call-me-heena-1.

--- "Call Me Heena." *The Daily Star* (London), March 4, 2017, https://
www.thedailystar.net/star-weekend/shutterstories/call-me-heena-1369819.

--- "Call Me Heena." Shahria Sharmin | Photographer. Accessed October 12,
2020. https://www.shahriasharmin.com/

--- "Call Me Heena: The Third Gender, Hijra - Photographs and Text by Shahria
Sharmin." *LensCulture*, 2017, www.lensculture.com/articles/shahria-sharmin-
call-me-heena-the-third-gender-hijra.

--- "The Dual Lives of Hijras in Bangladesh." *The Caravan*, June 30, 2017.

---https://caravanmagazine.in/photo-essay/hijras-bangaldesh-photos-shahria
-sharmin. "Shahria Sharmin." *LensCulture*. Accessed March 25, 2020. https://
www.lensculture.com/shahria-sharmin.

Stenqvist, Tove. "The Social Struggle of Being HIJRA in Bangladesh-cultural
Aspiration between Inclusion and Illegitimacy." Malmö: Malmö University,
2015.

Stief, Matthew. "The Sexual Orientation and Gender Presentation of Hijra,
Kothi, and Panthi in Mumbai, India." *Archives of Sexual Behavior* 46, no. 1
(January 2017): 73–85. https://doi.org/10.1007/s10508-016-0886-0

Walsh, Catherine E. "The Decolonial For: Resurgences, Shifts, and Movements."
In *On Decoloniality: Concepts, Analytics, Praxis* by Catherine E. Walsh and
Walter Mignolo, 15–32. New York City: Duke University Press, 2020. https://
doi.org/10.1515/9780822371779-003

PART 2: EMBODYING INTERSECTIONALITY

Chapter Five
Liberated from the Binary: An Interrogation of Gender in Rivers Solomon's *An Unkindness of Ghosts* and *The Deep*

Sandra Jacobo
Penn State University

Abstract

The chapter explores Rivers Solomon's queering of distinguished knowledges of the gender binary. Drawing on Black Feminist epistemologies, this book chapter examines how *An Unkindness of Ghosts* (2017) and *The Deep* (2019) engage in conversations that broaden our understanding of gender, Blackness, and embodiment. In the examination of these concepts, I connect Spillers's concept of "ungendering" to describe how Black women have been used for strenuous labor that would be assigned to cisgender men. I argue that Rivers Solomon's novels use the action of "ungendering" to criticize how societal structures utilize gender to delineate and restrict their citizens. In addition to issues of how gender is socialized, I write about the intersectional struggles each protagonist faces in their respective societies: Aster is aboard a generation spaceship, the *Matilda HSS*, which replicates the horrors of the antebellum past, while Yetu is part of an underwater society made up of descendants of pregnant enslaved Africans who were thrown overboard during the Transatlantic Slave Trade. In both works, Solomon builds worlds that are grounded in the realities of our own, where anti-Blackness and colonialism play major parts in the development and fracture of societies. I argue that Solomon implements Black Feminist embodied knowledges that allow readers to envision how fracture can create pathways to liberated worlds.

Keywords: Binary, Black Women, Embodiment, Black Feminism.

***

Introduction: Binaries in Society

The gender binary is so entrenched in modern Western society that it has become a distinct institution, producing regulation and oppression. The enforcement of gender is facilitated by "culturally formed discourses [that help] people [to] quickly decipher another's person's sex/gender as they grow up" (Cordoba 2023, 3). To be clear, quick deciphering of gender occurs at all stages of a person's life and is based on assumptions made solely from physical appearance and behaviors recognized as either male or female. Furthermore, quick deciphering acts as a form of gender policing by imposing rigid Eurocentric expectations of gender performance and roles. Misogyny and gender prejudice exist to maintain power for the masculine, and the gender binary functions to control all individuals who do not conform to its rules. The binary convinces society that gender operates dichotomously, with one's gender understood only in opposition to the other. This binary perspective, analogous to the binary racial categories of Black and white, fails to represent the embodied experiences of marginalized populations who have been harmed by this institution and others. Such binary ideas of gender extend beyond quick deciphering, enforcing control through ontological surveillance. One example is the rise of anti-LGBTQ+ laws that prohibit trans and gender nonconforming people from using public restroom spaces that most align with their gender identity. The binary, here, regulates by emphasizing the [non]presence of one's reproductive organs as the sole indicator of gender identity. This conflation not only reduces a person's value to their reproductive capability but also excludes and dismisses the experiences of cisgender individuals who have undergone surgeries such as hysterectomies or vasectomies. Ontological surveillance functions as an appendage of the gender binary, adhering to Eurocentric ideals of gender and race that assign white men and women as exemplars of each identity marker. Fundamentally, the gender binary inflicts harm across all gender and racial embodied experiences, but Black women, femme and non-binary persons endure the most harm due to the complex histories of their embodied experiences.

The Middle Passage marks the beginning of the Transatlantic Slave Trade, but also the start of one of the most egregious acts of social manipulation: ungendering. To ensure the success of this societal shift, Slave Trade powerbrokers used the ocean as a modality to wash away the established identities of the kidnapped. Omise'eke Natasha Tinsley expands on this in "Black Atlantic, Queer Atlantic: Queer Imaginings of the Middle Passage" (2008), where she notes that captured Africans were rendered "sexless and otherwise unmarked bodies that emerge as the legacy of geographically and historically specific waters, the Atlantic of the Middle Passage. Their brown bodies are gender fluid not because they choose parodic proliferations but because" their previous identities and experiences were simply washed away on their oceanic journeys (Tinsley 2008, 209). Tinsley's work is part of a larger epistemological genealogy established by Hortense Spillers's theories in her 1987 foundational publication, "Mama's Baby, Papa's Maybe: An American Grammar Book." From the ocean birthed distorted re-imaginings of Black people that blurred the lines of gender: "African persons in the Middle Passage literally suspended in the oceanic... [often contain an] ... undifferentiated [gender] identity...Under these conditions, one is neither female, nor male, as both subjects are taken into 'account' as quantities" (Spillers 1987, 72). The treatment of the bodies of kidnapped Africans (and Indigenous people already living in the Western Hemisphere) was part of what Spillers identifies as the

> socio-political order [which used] ... the theft of the body... [as a] willful and violent...severing of the captive body from its motive will. Under these conditions, we lose at least gender difference... and the female body and the male body become a territory of cultural and political maneuver, not at all gender-related, gender-specific. (Spillers 1987, 67)

Ungendering was a tool for powerbrokers in the slave trade to dehumanize enslaved Africans, asserting that they were nothing more than chattel. Ungendering allowed powerbrokers to manipulate how the bodies of enslaved Africans could be utilized for anything that they desired. Alongside repetitive violence and force, ungendering was a significant component of the system that justified centuries of forced labor, bodily violation, and societal degradation. Despite the reduction of the Black femme body to mere flesh, Black women only became recognized as women when powerbrokers sexually violated them for their own pleasure and profit. Through this "grammar" lesson, the reader learns how the gender binary functions as an unstable entity, reverberating through the work that follows. Moya Bailey writes, "[e]nslaved Black women were simultaneously gendered and ungendered through the objectification of their anatomy, whether in the service of white women's health or being rendered as genderless laborers and property" (Bailey 2021, 18). From these experiences of maltreatment emerges foundational Black feminist work, from Sojourner Truth's "Ain't I a Woman" (1851) to the extensive network of Black feminist thought and its epistemologies (bell hooks, Hortense Spillers, Christina Sharpe, Samantha Pinto, and many others). Black feminist epistemologies are also intertwined with the ideation and execution of Black queer theory, as both disciplines seek to uncover erased narratives and histories of the past.

Black trans embodiment exists in a world that is not ready to support or embrace it. Given the painful history and ongoing presence of unmitigated violence against Black people globally, it is imperative to discuss how this violence affects Black trans women and femme individuals at alarming rates. In 2023, over thirty-two transgender and gender nonconforming people lost their lives to physical or gun violence. Among this documented group, 84% of the victims were people of color (POC), and 50% identified as Black trans women (Human Rights Campaign Foundation). Black queer theorists Treva Ellison, Kai M. Green, Matt Richardson, and C. Riley Snorton write in "We Got Issues: Toward a Black Trans*/Studies" (2017), "Black is a modifier that changes everything. The power of blackness to change all that comes after is part of its close relationship to death" (Ellison et al. 2017, 166). In their 2021 publication, *Black Trans Feminism*, Marquis Bey asserts that "[t]ransness unfixes gender from essentialist moorings and posits itself precisely as that unfixation, as a departure-from without the presumption of a stable destination, or indeed a departure that itself destabilizes destinational desires" (Bey 2021, 3). Together, these definitions illustrate just how dangerous life is for Black trans people, particularly Black trans femmes. Both terms signify marginalized experiences, implying a distance from mainstream society and its ideals. "Black" connotes darkness—both physical and metaphorical—and death, while "trans" suggests a deviation from predictability and conformity. C. Riley Snorton and Jin Haritaworn declare that the Black transgender body stands in defiance of societal understandings of productive citizenship, marked as an "unruly body, which only in death can be transformed or translated into the service of state power" (Snorton and Haritaworn 2022, 68). The Black trans femme body has been brutalized and murdered across the diaspora; however, the nation-states and governmental institutions intended to protect citizens often fail to prevent or prosecute these hate crimes. This chapter utilizes literary analysis alongside Black feminist epistemologies, as well as Black queer and trans theory, as theoretical frameworks to emphasize the social critique of racism, the gender binary, and intersectional oppression present in Rivers Solomon's writing.

Rivers Solomon's (they/them) novels, *An Unkindness of Ghosts* (2017) and *The Deep* (2019), both present fictional worlds that challenge the gender binary. These novels center Black femme (gender nonconforming) protagonists in societies deeply scarred by slavery, with the legacy of pain and trauma interwoven into each protagonist's [un]gendered experience. Aster, the Black, non-binary, and neurodivergent protagonist in *An Unkindness of Ghosts*, resides on the spaceship *Matilda HSS*. This ship's societal structure allegorizes the horrors of the antebellum past by perpetuating racial and class divisions through an alphabetical deck system that does not allow "low deckers" basic human rights and freedoms. Yetu, the protagonist from *The Deep*, is part of an undersea society whose members are descendants of enslaved Africans thrown overboard during the Middle Passage. The wajinru, Yetu's people, are hybrid beings who can breathe and live underwater, representing an occluded outcome of the Transatlantic Slave Trade. Although the protagonists are very different, they are both connected to the traumas and afterlives of slavery. Their racialized embodiment is further complicated by their divergence from the gender binary. This chapter incorporates the aforementioned historical and theoretical frameworks to comprehensively understand Solomon's goals in publishing these novels. Spillers's theoretical framework influences my reading of gender in these works, allowing me to connect the resistance displayed by Aster and other characters in *An Unkindness of Ghosts* to Marquis Bey's concept of "traniflesh." This term is a mixture of theoretical concepts: Spillers's "flesh" and Green and Ellison's "tranifesting," and it describes a subjectivity that is liberated from the social restraints of race and gender, not tethered to the body.

Bey confronts the harmful history of ungendering with a theoretical intervention:

> Because gender via hegemonic logics is predicated on being visible to the mind, being material, being biological, being an immutable substance, traniflesh, in getting outside of those walled enclosures that ultimately signify fallacies and arbitrariness, becomes the un/gendered. It is not gendered, nor strictly speaking ungendered, as the slash in un/gendering marks a necessary slight departure from Spillers by drawing readers' attention to the liberatory, uncapturable otherwise of flesh, of traniflesh. (Bey 2021, 68)

I connect Bey's concept of "traniflesh" to the goals of this chapter: Through analytical investigation, I argue that these literary projects display how the once inhumane act of ungendering can create opportunities for resistance, kinship, and re-definition. My analysis specifically examines the lived conditions of the characters in *An Unkindness of Ghosts*, as well as reveals how these same characters "actively ungender" themselves in order to survive and covertly protest societal restrictions. This chapter also investigates how historical practices of enslavement and ungendering affected the psyche and formation of hidden communities present in Solomon's *The Deep*, detailing the intergenerational traumatic effects of these practices. If race and gender are indeed social constructs enforced by fear and prejudice, I argue that these same constructs can be manipulated to aid in the survival and resistance of Black trans femme and gender nonconforming individuals. I emphasize the significance of Solomon's speculative works in proposing ideas for a more just society for Black femme and gender nonconforming persons. I contend that, in both novels, Solomon utilizes and confronts the history of ungendering to create realities in which readers can recognize how resistance and healing can occur when gender is liberated from binary constructions.

The Role of Genre

The term 'speculative fiction' has been defined as a distinct category since the mid-twentieth century, often used interchangeably with 'science fiction.' It was initially defined in 1947 as "involving extrapolation from known science and technology," but later, in 1966, expanded to include stories focusing on "social change without necessarily [emphasizing] science or technology" (SF Encyclopedia 2017, 1-2). Less than thirty years later, Mark Dery coined the term, "Afrofuturism," which has been redefined by Ytasha Womack as "an intersection of imagination, technology, the future, and liberation... Afrofuturists redefine culture and notions of blackness... [by blending] ... elements of science fiction, historical fiction, speculative fiction, fantasy, Afrocentricity, and magic realism with non-Western beliefs" (Womack 2013, 9). As scholarly and popular attention to Afrofuturism and Black Speculative fiction increases, more Black narratives of survival and resistance are being published and discussed in both social circles.

In *Conversations with Nalo Hopkinson* (2022), prolific and foundational Black Caribbean author, Hopkinson describes how speculative fiction "forces [the reader] to think twice and thrice about a whole bunch of things in relation to each other: sexuality, race, class, color, history" (Lavender 2022, 14). Like Hopkinson, Rivers Solomon's novels engage with this writing tradition by presenting futures and alternate realities that challenge the many barriers Black queer people face in their communities. In fact, both Solomon's *The Deep* (2019) and Hopkinson's *New Moon Arms* (2004) connect the trauma of the Middle Passage to their mermaid lore, and this lore presents disruption to Western hierarchical societies (Davis 2021, 350). Solomon's writing is part of a legacy that both Ytasha Womack (2013) and Sami Schalk (2018) describe in their scholarship. In *Bodyminds Reimagined: (Dis)ability, Race and Gender in Black Women's Speculative Fiction* (2018), Schalk affirms that "[c]ontemporary black women's speculative fiction changes the rules of reality to create worlds with new or different genders, races, dis-abilities, and other forms of life, and in doing so these texts also require a change in how we read and interpret these categories" (Schalk 2018, 3). This genre of Black women's writing presents the capability of expanding literary classroom discussions to include prominent Black, Caribbean, gender, queer, and disability studies scholarship.

Toppling Stratified Order

Solomon's novel *An Unkindness of Ghosts* revisits and reckons with the troubled past of anti-Blackness and enslavement through the allegory of a spacecraft in a distant future, several hundred years from the present moment. Aster, a studied community healer, is trying to solve the mystery of her mother's death. As this task looms over her trajectory in the text, the reader is met with the living conditions of the lower-class residents. Solomon illustrates that time and trauma work congruently, in a cyclical fashion, by crafting the *Matilda HSS* as a mirror of the socioeconomic structure of historical slave colonies in the pre-twentieth-century Americas. The spaceship is divided into multiple decks, arranged in alphabetical order. For example, the A-deck and subsequent decks house the rich and privileged high-deck society, while decks Q to Z accommodate the low-deck society, which consists of Black sharecroppers surveilled by overseers and guards who often dehumanize them. This antebellum societal structure imitates the horrors and traumas of slavery. As the reader learns more about *Matilda*, it is evident that the realities Solomon depicts in the novel are meant to narrate that, without societal change, the past repeats itself.

Solomon describes a mass journey venturing through space for over 300 years to find a prophesied promised land/planet. This journey transcends centuries and generations of people, and yet, in the low decks, this journey proves to be an offshoot (and continuation) of the Middle Passage. In an interview with *The Rumpus*, Solomon states that "[e]ven the name, [Matilda,] … is based on Clotilde, the last known ship to carry enslaved people to the United States" (Watkins 2017, 9). Solomon enacts a history lesson in their narration of the Tarlander experience. Within Matildan society, the Tarlanders work as sharecroppers in human-made fields where they are abused in multiple ways by the guards who act as overseers. Breaking down the term "Tarlander," the word splits into three parts: "tar," "land," and the suffix "-er." The term "land" is defined, according to Merriam Webster, as a "solid part of the surface of the earth," which is a concept foreign to those aboard the ship, as no one has set foot on real land for generations. The suffix "-er" signals that these individuals work with or on land, while "tar," a thick black substance, evokes the color associated with the people on the lower decks. The racialized association is clear: Tarlanders, described in varying shades of brown, reflect the experiences of Black people in the reader's world. Aster, as a character, experiences multiple intersecting oppressions, with her Blackness dictating her social status and confinement to the lower decks. Following her mother's death, Aster is moved to the Q deck by a guard, citing "the peculiarities of Aster's physiology" (Solomon 2017, 35). In *Matilda*'s rigid society, her physical traits become the basis for discrimination. From the outset, readers witness how racial embodiment determines one's fate on the ship. Since the invention of race during the transatlantic slave trade, bodies have served as the primary markers of racial difference. As Solomon suggests, Black bodies—whether of women, men, or children—remain vulnerable to danger because of their physical appearance. Claudia Rankine's essay, "*The Condition of Black Life is One of Mourning*" (2015), articulates this persistent violence:

Dead [B]lacks are a part of normal life here. Dying in ship hulls, tossed into the Atlantic, hanging from trees, beaten, shot in churches, gunned down by the police or warehoused in prisons: Historically, there is no quotidian without the enslaved, chained or dead black body to gaze upon or to hear about or to position a self against. (Rankine 2015, 5)

The normalized violence Rankine describes—prevalent in both historical and contemporary contexts—finds echoes in Solomon's depiction of the Tarlanders, who anticipate violence as part of their daily existence. Solomon emphasizes the lived experiences of the marginalized to challenge complacency in societal attitudes toward the humanity of Black people.

Within the rigid social structure of *Matilda*, gender is defined by physical embodiment, reinforcing Eurocentric ideals. The ship's high-deck society expects men to dominate public life while women are confined to the household, expected to remain silent and chaste. However, the Tarlanders, subjected to forced labor and sexual violence, cannot conform to these norms. Their bodies, especially those of Tarlander women, are labeled as "queer" because they exist outside the parameters of Eurocentric femininity. Solomon explains how this bodily nonconformity leads to further marginalization: "Tarlander bodies did not always present as clearly male and female... This explained Aster's hairiness and muscular build despite being born with" external organs that produce estrogen and progesterone (Solomon 2017, 20). Here, Solomon highlights how the physical traits of Tarlander women, such as excess hair and muscle, are deemed unattractive and unfeminine by Eurocentric standards. The discrimination Tarlander women experience parallels the struggles faced by Black women in the present, who are often seen as failing to embody traditional femininity. This portrayal evokes the experience of enslaved Africans during the Middle Passage, where gender distinctions were erased under the brutality of enslavement. Samantha Pinto, in "Black Feminist Literacies: Ungendering, Flesh, and Post-Spillers Epistemologies of Embodied and Emotional Justice" (2017), elucidates this process:

Spillers argues for the site of the Middle Passage as a process of ungendering where Black bodies are erased of past gender-social identities and made into flesh. Though of course African women and men are still selected and differentially sexed and sexualized even in the architecture of the slave prison and the slave ship's hold, Spillers's ungendering is perhaps best pressed on as a radical differentiation in America's static but quite specifically formed notion of gendering that denotes Whiteness as the base of a normative process. (Pinto 2017, 27)

Here, Pinto describes the social logic of ungendering and, much like the static notion of gendering within the American imaginary, Matildans adhere to the same principles of upholding whiteness as the exemplar for proper gender norms. Like Black people, the Tarlanders' physical bodies do not align with these Eurocentric ideals, which becomes a justification for their oppression. This ideology is reinforced by influential figures aboard the ship, who proclaim: "[The] Tarlanders were not of the Heavens. Even beasts of the field were made male and female, were they not? So, they might multiply and spread the Heavens' bounty. Tarlanders did not come male and female—everything but" (Solomon 2017, 19). Like the slave ships in the Middle Passage, Solomon likens this ideology to the notions created by the crew and slaveholders about the kidnapped Africans. This action of ungendering Tarlanders contradicts itself in many ways, and it is specifically crafted to fit the desires of the high deck residents and government to maintain societal hierarchies. However, Aster's embodiment and ability to stealthily resist the Matildan law enforcement gestures to the liberating potential of ungendering.

Aster engages in active ungendering as an act of resistance by preventing her body from perpetuating the curse of non-belonging and non-being to future offspring: She elects to undergo a hysterectomy. In the novel, Solomon positions Aster's decision as a direct challenge to Matildan societal structures. For Aster, the hysterectomy removes her ability to give birth, and this loss of reproductive capacity grants her agency over her own body. As mentioned in the introduction of this chapter, a hysterectomy does not negate the gender identities or embodied knowledge of cisgender women. However, in the novel, this surgery symbolizes resistance. This act of defiance counters the inherited trauma of the Middle Passage and slavery while also aligning with historical acts of resistance by enslaved Black women, who sometimes killed their newborn children, either by throwing them overboard ships or covertly ending their lives on plantations. Solomon portrays this moment as one of liberation and positivity, opening Chapter IV with distinctive fairy-tale language: "Once upon a time, Theo removed Aster's uterus. He made her breathe air that wasn't air. When she awoke, all that remained of her womb was a ghost" (Solomon 2017, 43). This juxtaposition between fairy tale exposition within the grave reality of this antebellum society reveals to the reader the rarity of happiness and joy for low-deck residents. Theo, the Surgeon General, allied with Aster, liberates Aster from the organs that classify her as female. And in this moment, Aster feels relief as she finally breathes in the air of a world that can no longer burden her with the responsibility of child rearing. In this environment, where her body is constantly monitored and controlled, Aster's choice marks a rejection of societal expectations. No longer "capable of carrying offspring," Aster is declared, according to "Matilda's manifest[,] ... Fit to Breed" (Solomon 2017, 43). The use of the word breed exemplifies how Matildan society reduces

Aster's body to a reproductive tool for the labor system. This term serves as yet another reminder of how the Tarlanders are dehumanized, regarded as animals whose purpose is to serve the system, much like how enslaved Black people were exploited in the development of Western economies.

In *Ain't I a Woman: Black Women and Feminism* (1981), bell hooks identifies this issue: "[white people's] lack of interest and concern deliberately minimizes the black female slave experience...the black female was exploited as a laborer in the fields, a worker in the domestic household, a breeder and as an object of white male sexual assault" (hooks 1981, 22). bell hooks deciphers the social code of the *Matilda*: The Tarlanders are often ungendered and dehumanized in order to justify the frequent abuse they face. Not only are these Tarlander workers expected to perform at an efficient, speedy rate, but the female population was also subjected to relentless attempts at sexual assault. Aster's refusal to continue this legacy displays Solomon's intentions to highlight the perverse and violent nature of a gender binary that supports conceptualizing Black people as flesh. However, it is not only low-deck populations who can benefit from active ungendering.

Surgeon General Theo Smith is another character who finds his own agency through subtle acts of ungendering. Through Theo's recollections of his childhood, the reader is confronted with the prevalent queerphobia within Matildan society. Theo muses, "[m]y sissyness and my sickliness were two sides of the same coin to my father... The scandal of my birth—bastard child of a [B]lack woman—had already forced his resignation as sovereign. The least I could do was be a good and strapping lad" (Solomon 2017, 99). Solomon reveals that even though Theo is not a low-deck resident, he is still burdened by his Black parentage. His racial composition complicates how he might carry on his family's legacy. Although Theo's Blackness is not legible to Matildan society, it represents a source of dysfunction for his father. This is because Theo embodies his father's indiscretion—his relationship with a Tarlander woman—thereby becoming a symbol of shame. To draw the reader's attention to the complex realities of embodiment, Solomon deliberately obscures the legibility of Theo's race, emphasizing the ableist nature of Matilda. Theo's chronic illness presents an uncontrollable embodiment that challenges his father's expectations and complicates his gender performance. Societal understandings of masculinity and manhood are connected to physical strength and agility, which are oppositional depictions of Theo's embodiment. In consideration of Theo's chronic illness and gender performance, Solomon displays that, despite his rank as Surgeon General, Theo is still subject to scrutiny and violence in this society.

Solomon displays how resistance happens in high-deck society through Theo's covert and cunning forms of resistance. Theo utilizes his access to Aster's alternative medicine to treat his post-poliomyelitis syndrome[1] because "it's a testosterone antagonist" (Solomon 2017, 100). And while it keeps him looking younger, it also keeps him from growing a beard. Theo's ability to move through the alphabetical structure of the ship without assistance is due to his whiteness and his father's high status. However, Solomon shows that, to avoid bodily violence, Theo must navigate the decks carefully and strategically, ensuring he does not upset or provoke the guards. Theo leverages his knowledge of religious traditions to deviate from expectations of masculine embodiment, though members of high-deck society regard him with suspicion: "My earrings, though religious in nature, are a practice most other high deck men have long ago abandoned. I have three black dots under each of my eyes, drawn there with a coal pencil. It is religious, but they know that I am off" (Solomon 2017, 108). While Theo expresses his piety by building altars and praying regularly, his resistance lies in using religious tradition to adopt feminine adornments, challenging gender norms. Kamri Jordan affirms that "Theo utilizes religion in a rejection of the gender binary. Theo finds liberation through this subversion" (Jordan 2022, 29). This subversion is an example of active ungendering, as Theo employs unique knowledge to resist Matildan ideals surrounding gender and race. Solomon's inclusion of Theo's trauma from his upbringing serves as a key factor in his collaboration with Aster to form queer kinship.

Due to this collaboration, Aster gains access to the upper deck of the ship. Along with assisting Aster in her hysterectomy, Theo provides her with new clothes, shoes, and a haircut to make her gender performance convincing enough to protect her from interrogation, harm, and removal. Solomon writes, "The haircut, contrary to her initial fear, had unlatched and freed her. She ran her fingers over the neatly shorn strands. It was lovely and exquisite" (Solomon 2017, 212). In this moment, Aster feels liberated because her hair was connected to a gender identity and embodiment that she did not resonate with. The weight and presence of her strands signaled femininity to Matildan society, but it also marked the perpetual danger that Tarlander (Black) women face. Similar to the relief she experienced after her hysterectomy, Aster finds agency through gender imperceptibility. Now presenting as Aston, she accompanies Theo to the high-deck celebration—the coronation of the new sovereign— where multiple executions will occur "in order...[to] maintain a level of decorum" (Solomon 2017, 217). In this scene, Aster observes and absorbs how order is maintained in Matildan society. Solomon creates a juxtaposition between Aston and a fellow low-deck woman who wears "a head wrap... [and] a chain around her ankle attached to a weight" (Solomon 2017, 219). This

---

[1] Post-poliomyelitis syndrome (PPS) is a condition that causes gradual muscle weakness and muscle atrophy (loss) that can affect people who've had polio.

contrasting image highlights how Aster defies a societal structure that only allows low-deck women access to the upper decks in bondage. With Theo's support, Aster obscures her physical gendered embodiment to navigate the ship more easily than other shipmates who share her phenotype. Theo and Aster resist the ship's oppressive structure by deciding for themselves "what [their] bodies are or are not" (Solomon 2017, 308). Through their resistance, Solomon emphasizes the intersectional complexities of the experiences of Black women and femme people. The novel offers an intriguing perspective on the historical practice of ungendering and explores how it can be used to resist societal structures rather than reinforce them.

Deep in Genderless Communities

Solomon's *The Deep* (2019) centers on the wajinru (which means "chorus of the sea"), descendants of Africans who drowned during the Middle Passage. These hybrid creatures, with fins instead of legs, possess the ability to breathe underwater. Yetu, the wajinru historian and protagonist, is the sole member of her society who holds over 600 years of collective memory and trauma, starting from the birth of the first wajinru. The immense burden of this traumatic history causes Yetu's mental and physical health to deteriorate. Overwhelmed, she flees from her responsibilities just before the annual Remembrance Ceremony, a tradition where the Historian shares the community's collective trauma for a brief period so that the wajinru can reclaim a sense of belonging. Afterward, the Historian takes back the memories and history until the next ceremony, allowing the community to live unburdened. This novella takes readers on a journey of self-discovery for Yetu, where she learns to find balance between serving others and caring for herself.

The Deep is a collaboration between Rivers Solomon and the experimental hip-hop group, clipping., which consists of Daveed Diggs (American actor and rapper), William Hutson (musical artist), and Jonathan Snipes (musical composer). The novella was inspired by clipping.'s electronic rap song, "The Deep," from which Solomon drew themes related to the ocean, sea life, and ancestral connections to pregnant African women thrown overboard during the Middle Passage. In essence, the collaborators created a sonic and literary re-imagining of Spillers's theories. Through both these sonic and literary narratives, the story of the wajinru becomes deeply tied to the trauma of the Middle Passage and the compounded oppression experienced by Africans and their descendants. Solomon emphasizes the devastating truth of the many lives lost, traumatized, or otherwise impacted by the horrific conditions aboard slave ships. Because of the violence inflicted upon Black people globally, their bodies are often perceived as "carriers of terror" in contemporary Western society (Sharpe 2016, 19). Ontologically, the presence of Black people serves as a reminder of Western society's "continuing need to destroy flesh for the preservation of social order" (Pinn 2003, 78). This is exemplified by the ongoing violence against Black trans people, particularly Black trans femme individuals, without judicial or societal intervention. Even though Black people are not the perpetrators of this violence, their lived experiences remain marked by the constant threat of harm. However, Solomon refuses to dwell solely on danger, terror, and pain. In an interview with *Lightspeed Magazine*, Solomon states:

> While the Trans-Atlantic Slave Trade was happening, there was a whole, vast world happening outside of it. This phenomenon that has become a foundation of how the modern world is structured was just . . . boats. I do not know if I have anything useful or important to say about that, other than that it's gutting. We have all of this raw material around us, full of potential—wood, steel . . . people—and so often, this raw material has, instead of being transformed into beauty, been mutated into traumas. Coming from this pain, the wajinru are very concerned with building a life under the sea that's wondrous rather than catastrophic. Part of this is witnessing the ships that originated them. (Solomon 2019, 10)

Through this mode of travel, colonizing forces expanded their empires without a second thought about the devastating realities unfolding aboard these ships. During the Middle Passage, there was a sense of wonder at how these vessels carried fortune for some and generations of trauma for others. Solomon uses the word "gutting" in this passage, and I cannot help but connect this metaphorical use to the ways that the powerbrokers of the Transatlantic Slave Trade also "gutted" the bodies, ideologies, and knowledge of the enslaved passengers to achieve their financial goals. In this reality, where, as Spillers describes, social and political maneuvering shaped these oppressive conditions, there was a heavy emphasis on sight to justify these social hierarchies. Just as enslaved Africans endured and adapted to compounded traumas on land, Solomon imagines a world where such trauma transforms into a liberation from the burden of visual difference.

Solomon confronts this mode of differentiation by removing sight as the primary sensory function in the wajinru society. The wajinru live deep in the ocean, where darkness compromises their vision, forcing them to rely on physical touch and sensation to survive. Even though touch is key to the wajinru's embodied experience, Solomon uses Yetu's perspective to immerse the reader in the overwhelming nature of physical contact in the ocean. Through touch, the wajinru navigate their underwater world. Painfully disconnected from their mothers and any knowledge of their ancestral background, generations of wajinru have roamed the ocean guided only by touch. This sense enables them to locate orphaned pups by following ships that cross the Atlantic. Touch also serves as a major form of communication, instead of speech, the wajinru "communicate how pups communicate. In electricity, in charges." (Solomon 2019, 63). The wajinru embrace the currents above and below to locate others like themselves, using touch as a language. Through this sensory modality, Solomon's focus on touch and feeling functions to negate Eurocentric ideals, showing the hypocrisy of the Transatlantic Slave Trade taking place during the Age of Enlightenment. The Historian learns, experiences, and transfers the history of the wajinru. Consequently, the role of Historian demands a high level of sensitivity to handle the weight of this task. Yetu's experience offers a critique of the reliance on physical touch within the wajinru community:

> Most of the time, Yetu kept her senses dulled. As a child, she'd learned to shut out what she could of the world, lest it overwhelm her into fits. But now she had to open herself back up, to make her body a wound again... Yetu closed her eyes and honed in on the vibrations of the deep, purposefully resensitizing her scaled skin to the onslaught of the circus that is the sea. (Solomon 2019, 2)

Yetu's experience presents that, although the wajinru does not adhere to the gender binary, it is not without flaws. Yetu's character is neurodivergent, and this representation is important to the plot overall. Ada Hoffman, in "Autistic Book Party, Episode 60: *The Deep*," writes, "[m]ore sensitive than other historians due to her neurotype, she struggles intensely" (Hoffman 2020, 5). Her struggle reveals how the community has failed to fully process the pain and trauma from its past. With heightened sensitivity to touch, Yetu illustrates how the tradition of the Historian can harm both the individual in that role and the community as a whole. Her journey allows readers to grasp the importance of honoring embodied knowledge through touch. Solomon's emphasis on touch as a literary device serves as a form of resistance against the continued violence inflicted on Black bodies. Ideological and physical violence against Black people has historically been used to impose social order throughout the Transatlantic Slave Trade. Sowande' M. Mustakeem describes this violence as functioning "as a shared language through which bonds people were routinely victimized" (Mustakeem 2016, 77). This treatment connected the worth of Black individuals to the exploitation of their bodies. The Middle Passage, as Mustakeem elaborates, created a framework that justified mistreatment by distorting perceptions of Black bodies—perceptions that persisted for centuries and continue into the present day. Iman Cooper underscores this commodification of Black bodies:

> Depriving humans of dignity, agency, respect, and basic human rights
> was also the tool that was later used by slave-owners in order to create
> and maintain the inferior slave subject. Essentially, the humanity of the
> black body was ruptured into an object to be bought and sold, in order
> to satisfy the economic desires of the white slave owners. (Cooper 2015,
> 23)

Because Black bodies were forcibly reduced to objects, Western society inscribed them with meaning through acts of violence. In response, Black individuals developed strategies of survival that included suppressing outward expressions of pain. This necessary performance of desensitization led to the stereotype that Black bodies were inherently more resilient than white bodies, contributing to Western society's desensitization to Black suffering. As the powerbrokers of the Transatlantic Slave Trade desensitized themselves from understanding and registering the pain they inflicted on Black bodies, this desensitization also resulted in how Black people viewed themselves. This feeling led to powerlessness and encouraged the disconnection between Black people and their bodies.

This theme of desensitization echoes in Yetu's struggle with her role as Historian. The overstimulation of the ocean's environment makes it unsafe for one person to bear the burden of ancestral memories and pain alone. Through Yetu, the reader gains insight into the structure of the wajinru community and its limitations. The novel suggests that even marginalized communities, like the wajinru, are not immune to placing harmful expectations on their members. Solomon challenges the idea that such communities can escape the intersectional oppressions embedded in their histories.

The History of the wajinru cannot be remembered as a community because their pasts and origins are far too traumatic. Most wajinru live in happy ignorance, while the Historian, the keeper of collective memory, bears the physical and emotional pain of the past. The Remembrance, a ceremony held once a year, allows the wajinru community to learn about their ancestral background and history. During the ceremony, the Historian shares these memories with the community to help them understand and connect with the past. As descendants of enslaved Africans who were brutalized and systematically oppressed for centuries, the wajinru carry the pain as both a reminder of the dangerous world of the "two legs" and a way to connect with their ancestors. As a literary device for representing generational trauma, Solomon uses the reenactment of bodily pain to retell the wajinru's history:

> [Yetu] felt her whole body go rigid and snap. Her body was full of other
> bodies. Every wajinru who had ever lived possessed her in this moment.

They gnashed, they clawed, desperate to speak. Yetu channeled their memories, sore and shaking as she brought them to the surface. The shock of it nearly knocked her unconscious. She had once imagined… the past running gently through her. It was more like slitting an opening in herself so they could get out. (Solomon 2019, 28)

This passage illustrates how Yetu experiences the pain of bodies that existed before her birth. As a community leader, she guides the wajinru on a time-traveling journey. Moving through time periods and communal memory, Yetu resurfaces and re-experiences shared trauma to facilitate healing within the group. In her role as Historian, Yetu symbolically takes on a maternal role by "birthing" the memories of her community, initiating a cyclical process that can be described as the rebirth of the wajinru. Yetu's struggle with this maternal role reflects how society fails to support mothers who are Black women and femme people. In the real world, Black women have historically been viewed not as nurturers to their own children but as reproducers of labor for their enslavers. Solomon critiques these restrictive ideas of motherhood through the role of the Historian. Yetu's experience strips away any glamour associated with the maternal role, exposing the burden of the responsibility she carries. Over time, the wajinru community grows through shared experiences of loss and disorientation, transforming pain into communal kinship. However, since the burden of their origin story resides within one individual at any given time, the Historian is often isolated from the community, creating tension and misunderstanding within this seemingly utopian space.

The complex power dynamic between Yetu and her mother, Amaba, is exacerbated by Yetu's role as Historian, as she becomes the sole bearer of ancestral knowledge. This creates a disparity between them: Although Amaba is proud of Yetu's societal role, she fails to acknowledge her suffering. As Yetu's traumatic memories come and go, she falls into trances, distancing herself from her role. Through this experience, she confronts, receives, and suffers the trauma of the past. Yetu's relationship with Amaba reveals the miscommunication within the wajinru community. Solomon writes:

"Without answers, there is only a hole… where a history should be… We are cavities. You don't know what it's like, blessed with the rememberings as you are," said Amaba. Yetu did know what it was like. After all, wasn't cavity just another word for vessel? Her own self had been scooped out when she was a child of fourteen years to make room for ancestors, leaving her empty and wandering and ravenous. (Solomon 2019, 8)

In this exchange, Amaba explains the wajinru's struggle. Without access to their ancestral memory, the wajinru feel empty, like cavities devoid of substance or a past. However, what Amaba and the community do not realize is that Yetu feels a similar emptiness, despite holding all the ancestral memories within her. Solomon's use of the term "vessel" functions as a double entendre, replacing Amaba's "cavity." The role of Historian strips Yetu of her individuality, turning her into an empty vessel for collective memory, echoing how the practice of ungendering reduced Black women to flesh and vessels was used to fulfill the goals of their enslavers.

The Historian's role carries too much trauma and physical pain. Yetu's discontent with this role reflects Solomon's critique of how marginalized communities can impose unrealistic expectations on their members. The wajinru do not live in a utopia free from intersectional oppression. Similarly, Black femme identities are often romanticized, with their strength idealized while ignoring the reality of having to endure constant oppression (hooks 1981, 6). Pressured by her community's expectations, Yetu flees to a small body of water near an unnamed piece of land, seeking refuge from the ocean. During this self-imposed exile, Yetu meets Oori, an orphan and the sole survivor of her people. Oori represents a lesson for Yetu. When she learns about Yetu's abandonment of her community, Oori responds: "I would take any amount of pain in the world if it meant I could know all the memories of the Oshuben" (Solomon 2019, 94). The Oshuben were a small group of families native to the land where Yetu meets Oori, and Oori is the last of her kin. Oori's words emphasize the importance of embracing the traumatic past to build community, while Yetu advocates for change that prioritizes self-care and mental health. The conflict between the two characters highlights how trauma has shaped their lives in distinct ways. Yet, because their traumas are rooted in the same system of slavery, Solomon creates a path toward kinship between them. Yetu, as Historian, initiates Oori into the wajinru community:

> [Yetu and Oori] held each other close until Yetu was able to transfer to Oori the remembering of the womb. Lost in it, Oori stopped treading, and she sank a little... But when Oori jolted from the remembering, she was breathing underwater, just as she breathed in the womb. (Solomon 2019, 155)

In this scene, Yetu symbolically gives birth to a two-leg for the first time, enabling Oori to breathe and live in the ocean. Just as the wajinru's origin story tells of abandoned beings finding each other in the ocean's depths, Oori and Yetu forge a new connection. Though Oori was wandering alone on land, her disconnect from her people resembled the zoti aleyu who found their way to each other in the deep ocean. zoti aleyu was a previous name that the wajinru used to identify themselves. Through this small ceremony, Solomon suggests a hopeful solution: The wajinru can share their trauma collectively and continuously, distributing the burden across the community rather than leaving it to one person.

Conclusion

Within these two novels, Solomon creates narratives of characters, communities, and traumas connected to the act of ungendering. Various depictions of embodiment (occluded, defiant, and transformative) inform the reader of how uncontested racial and gender injustices abuse the body and generate intergenerational trauma. In both texts, the reader can distinguish how influential the practice of ungendering is to the physical body. In *An Unkindness of Ghosts*, Solomon demonstrates how ungendering has created environments that manipulate people and narratives to justify violence and violation. Solomon also displays how Aster and Theo enact ungendering through their own manipulation to resist the societal structures of the *Matilda*. In *The Deep*, the historical harm of ungendering creates a new species, persistent in nature but also traumatized by the disregard of their ancestors' bodies. Even though the wajinru society and consciousness seem to be divorced from many two-leg cultural constructions of gender, race, and division, Solomon adeptly exhibits how legacies (colonialism, slavery, and ungendering, specifically) affect and shape the dysfunction of their community. Here, ungendering creates new forms of embodiment that transform into something promising and divergent from the past. Through both instances, the reader imagines communities existing in defiance of the gender binary. However, as scholars, we cannot sever these experiences of gender expression from the historical context of the Middle Passage and slavery. Spillers's theory of ungendering highlights the horrors that were justified through manipulation, but her theory also exposes how this act erased preexisting gender identities that existed in many African nations before European contact. Same-sex marriages were common in over 40 precolonial societies throughout the continent, encouraging effeminate men to marry other men and prosperous women to marry multiple women (Elnaiem 2021, par. 2). This historical instance predates the Middle Passage, but it challenges established notions of the gender binary. Seeing this historical example of gender performance from ancestral African cultural traditions helps the reader understand how gender functions differently outside of the Western imagination. In consideration of using the Middle Passage as a framework to critique societal delineations, Solomon informs their readers that history will only repeat itself if society does not work towards eliminating the intersectional oppressions that Black femme people endure. By highlighting important Black queer and femme narratives, Solomon challenges Western social practices of policing Black femme bodies. Solomon's work with queer embodiment, specifically with their attention to non-binary experiences, not only challenges preconceived notions of gender but highlights the interconnectivity of gender to race and class in the same ways that Akwaeke Emezi considers gender identity and mental health in their 2018 publication, *Freshwater* (Mutton 2023, 23). In addition, by challenging these societal standard fictions, Solomon's writing encourages other Black queer writers to write and live for their liberation. Considering this, I dedicate this chapter in commemoration of the lives of Diamond Brigman, A'nee Johnson, De'Vonnie J'Rae Johnson, Lisa Love, and countless others whose names are often erased from mainstream Western media.

Bibliography

Bailey, Moya. *Misogynoir Transformed: Black Women's Digital Resistance*. New York: New York University Press, 2021. https://doi.org/10.18574/nyu/9781479803392.001.0001

Bey, Marquis. *Black Trans Feminism*. Duke University Press, 2021. https://doi.org/10.1515/9781478022428

Cooper, Iman. "Commodification of the black body, sexual objectification and social hierarchies during slavery." *Earlham Historical Journal* 7, no. 2 (2015): 21-41.

Cordoba, Sebastian. *Non-binary Gender Identities: The Language of Becoming. Gender and Sexualities in Psychology*. Routledge, 2023. https://doi.org/10.4324/9781003120360

Davis, Jalondra A. "Crossing Merfolk, the Human, and the Anthropocene in Nalo Hopkinson's The New Moon's Arms and Rivers Solomon's The Deep." *Journal of the Fantastic in the Arts* 32, no. 3 (2021): 349-467.

Ellison, Treva, Kai M. Green, Matt Richardson, and C. Riley Snorton. "We Got Issues: Toward a Black Trans/Studies." *TSQ: Transgender Studies Quarterly* 4, no. 2 (2017): 162-169. https://doi.org/10.1215/23289252-3814949

Elnaiem, Mohammed. "The 'Deviant' African Genders That Colonialism Condemned" *JSTOR Daily*. 29 April 2021. https://daily.jstor.org/the-deviant-african-genders-that-colonialism-condemned/

Hoffman, Ada. "Autistic Book Party, Episode 60: *The Deep*." Ada Hoffman. 29 March 2020. https://www.ada-hoffmann.com/2020/03/29/autistic-book-party-episode-60-the-deep/

hooks, bell. *Ain't I a Woman: Black Women and Feminism*. Boston, MA: South End Press, 1981.

Human Rights Campaign. "Fatal Violence Against the Transgender and Gender-Expansive Community in 2023." Accessed 15 April 2024. https://www.hrc.org/resources/fatal-violence-against-the-transgender-and-gender-expansive-community-in-2023

Jordan, Kamri. "Bye Bye Binary: Reimagining Gender in *An Unkindness of Ghosts*." *CLA Journal* 65, no. 1 (2022): 23-31. https://doi.org/10.1353/caj.2022.0004

Lavender III, Isiah, ed. *Conversations with Nalo Hopkinson*. Univ. Press of Mississippi, 2022.

Mustakeem, Sowande M. *Slavery at Sea: Terror, Sex, and Sickness in the Middle Passage*. University of Illinois Press, 2016. https://doi.org/10.5406/illinois /9780252040559.001.0001

Mutton, Nicola. "Representation of Non-Binary Identities in Feminist Literature of the Early 21st Century: A Literary Critique." *Studies in Social Science & Humanities* 2, no. 12 (2023): 20-27. https://doi.org/10.56397 /SSSH.2023.12.04

Pinn, Anthony B. "Black bodies in pain and ecstasy: terror, subjectivity, and the nature of Black religion." *Nova religio* 7, no. 1 (2003) pp. 76-89. https://doi .org/10.1525/nr.2003.7.1.76

Pinto, Samantha. "Black Feminist Literacies: Ungendering, Flesh, and Post-Spillers Epistemologies of Embodied and Emotional Justice." *Journal of Black Sexuality and Relationships* 4, no. 1 (2017): 25-45. https://doi.org/10.1353/ bsr.2017.0019

Rankine, Claudia. "The Condition of Black Life Is One of Mourning." *The New York Times*. 2015. https://www.nytimes.com/2015/06/22/magazine/the-condition-of-black-life-is-one-of-mourning.html

Sharpe, Christina. *In the wake: On Blackness and Being*. Duke University Press, 2016. https://doi.org/10.1515/9780822373452

Snorton, C. Riley, and Jin Haritaworn. "Trans necropolitics: A transnational reflection on violence, death, and the trans of color afterlife." *The transgender studies reader remix*, pp. 305-316. Routledge, 2022. https://doi.org/10.4324/9 781003206255-33

Solomon, Rivers. *An Unkindness of Ghosts*. Akashic Books, 2017.

Solomon, Rivers. "Interview: Rivers Solomon." Interview by Christian A. Collins, *Lightspeed Magazine*, November, Issue 114. (2019). https://www.lightspeed magazine.com/nonfiction/interview-rivers-solomon/

Solomon, Rivers, Daveed Diggs, William Hutson, and Jonathan Snipes. *The Deep*. Simon and Schuster, 2019. eBook.

"Speculative Fiction." *SFE: Speculative Fiction*, September 15, 2017. https://sf-encyclopedia.com/entry/speculative_fiction.

Spillers, Hortense J. "Mama's Baby, Papa's Maybe: An American grammar book." *diacritics* 17, no. 2 (1987): 65-81. https://doi.org/10.2307/464747

Tinsley, Omise'eke Natasha. "Black Atlantic, Queer Atlantic: Queer Imaginings of the Middle Passage." *GLQ: A Journal of Lesbian and Gay Studies*, 14, no. 2-3 (2008): 191-215. https://doi.org/10.1215/10642684-2007-030

Watkins, Claire Vaye. "Magical Systems and Fusion Reactors: Rivers Solomon Discusses An Unkindness of Ghosts" *The Rumpus*, 26 September 2017. https: //therumpus.net/2017/09/26/the-rumpus-interview-with-rivers-solomon/

Womack, Ytasha L. *Afrofuturism: The world of black sci-fi and fantasy culture*. Chicago Review Press, 2013.

Chapter Six
Trans and Asexual Representation: Between Oversexualization and Dehumanization

Kayla Reed
Grinnell College

Abstract

The representation of LGBT+ individuals in the media has a long and evolving history. Media representation has had, and continues to have, a positive impact on society by fostering empathy, promoting understanding, and providing queer individuals with a sense of visibility and representation. But often, extremes are used to display queer characters to the masses, creating new stereotypes and myths. Stereotypes in media have proven harmful to many groups, as demonstrated by Castaneda (2018), Appel and Weber (2021), and ongoing studies. From the frequent "AIDS episode of the week" in the 1990s to the "Bury Your Gays" trope, where gay couples are denied happy endings, shallow and negative representation can have lasting consequences. But not having representation can be harmful as well, as the Trans and Asexual community knows. Providing a brief timeline for LGBT+ representation in US media with a focus on television and moving to streaming, the study will examine some of the best and worst examples of Trans and Asexual representation to date. Asexual and trans representation have an interesting parallel: Asexuals are depicted as being inhuman due to a lack of sexual interest, while Trans individuals are over-sexualized and depicted in a predatory manner. The best representation is emerging in children's shows, similar to the boom of good LGBT+ representation that has been seen in Young Adult novels. The study will also examine what elements are missing from existing representations and what improvements could be made.

Keywords: Stereotypes, Media, Television.

***

Introduction

In reviewing the history of media in the United States, the LGBT+ community holds a position that many minorities experience of seeing both incredible increases in representation and stagnation of that representation. In the early days of television and movies, LGBT+ characters were not common occurrences. Even after the Stonewall Riots, LGBT+ representation did not see real growth until the 1990s, almost twenty years later. As representation started to grow, the focus was primarily on white gay men. Other groups can see representation from time to time, but white gay men are the majority of LGBT+ characters (Moylan 2015). As a result, other groups, particularly those in the transgender and asexual communities, often struggle to achieve accurate and positive representation. Both representations have more significant variances from the social norm than gay men do. The asexual identity is newer than trans; the idea of a sexless being has been used in media to create an 'other' type of being. This trope is frequently seen in science fiction, often featuring robots and aliens. Between the transgender and asexual communities, we see the polarization of dehumanizing LGBT+ individuals either through over-sexualization or hypo-sexualization. Shallow representation reinforces these stereotypes and tropes, causing harm to individuals who identify with these groups (Appel and Weber 2021). Television and media must strive to create more diverse, authentic representations to help combat harmful stigmas and create more diverse storytelling.

Representation Regarding Culture and Minorities

All representations are shaped by the culture that produces them, whether in books, television, art, or other forms of media. In addition, representations influence the culture that consumes them. The creator and the interpreter define the importance of the representation. Hall affirmed,

> In part, we give things meaning by how we represent them- the words we use about them, the stories we tell about them, the images of them we produce, the emotions we associate with them, the ways we classify and conceptualize them, the values we place on them. Culture, we may say, is involved in all those practices that are not simply genetically programmed into us- like the jerk of a knee when tapped-but which carry meaning and value for us, which need to be meaningfully interpreted by others or which depend on meaning for their effective operation. (Hall 1997, 3)

Numerous studies have demonstrated how media representations shape public perceptions on various issues. Whether examining the portrayal of feminism in telenovelas (Acosta-Alzuru, 2003) or how young Black men form ideas of masculinity (Goodwill et al., 2019), representations are both a reflection of and a driving force behind the culture in which they are created and consumed.

Discussions around representation regarding minority populations are far from new. Clark (1969) defined four types of representation: non-recognition, ridicule, regulation, and respect. Berry identified three stages of representation for Black characters on television: The stereotypic era, the era of new awareness, and the era of stabilization (Berry, 1980). LGBT+ representation follows similar trajectories to those of other minority groups, though with variations in how it is portrayed. The most noticeable parallel today can be observed with white gay men, who have historically had the most representation. White gay men have experienced periods of non-recognition, ridicule, and regulation, but are now largely respected in mainstream media. Asexuality, being a relatively newer identity, is still in the early stages of representation, though depictions of sexless or non-sexual characters have appeared intermittently in US media. LGBT+ representation currently sits within the new awareness age in many respects, with exceptions for certain representations and intersectional identities.

Media History of LGBT+ In the United States

LGBT+ media representation could have had a better starting point. Although conversations and characters can be seen as early as the 1950s, a little over a decade after televisions started being sold commercially in the United States, the representation was not only minor but also detrimental. Before the 1960s is referred to as the non-recognition age, mixed with ridicule and influenced by the strong heteronormative values of the time. Light inclusion of gay content in movie theatres in the early 1960s led to inclusion in television, with LGBT+ individuals as the punchline (Caputso 2000, 4). The end of the 1960s saw the first development as TV began to appeal to the next generation using social issues such as the Sexual Revolution and feminism (Caputso 2000, 4). Capsuto states,

> In their quest to cash in on social controversies, some producers experimented with different ways to incorporate gay content into existing T.V. genres safely. Specific patterns quickly emerged and continued unchanged into the 1980s. Most of the gay characters were white men in their twenties or thirties. When a lesbian did appear, she was carrying a smoking gun or bloodied knife (Capsuto 2000, 4).

The 1970s was a significant decade for the LGBT+ community. The American Psychiatric Association removed homosexuality from the list of psychiatric disorders, and many other positive movements happened for the LGBT+ community (Rosen 2014). Due to so much happening, it was in the 1970s that the 'coming out script' became a common trope in television, as well as the more harmful 'gay monster' (Caputso 2013, 4-5). Gay characters became murderers and sexual predators. With LGBT+ characters already drenched in other stereotypes of the time, this would create a new stereotype age for the LGBT+ community. The transgender community experienced the worst of this. Abbott reviewed trans characters in the media, tracing the 'gay monster' epidemic regarding trans individuals. Abbott states:

> By the 1970s, an archetype of a violent trans criminal had become firmly entrenched in popular entertainment. Variations of this archetype appeared on the most popular television crime dramas of the 1970s and 1980s, from *The Streets of San Francisco* (ABC, 1974) and *Police Woman* (NBC, 1976) to *Magnum, P.I.* (CBS, 1982) and *T.J. Hooker* (ABC, 1984). These psychotic mass murderers impersonated nuns or nurses to target women but were ultimately "exposed" as men, often with a dramatic wig reveal. (Abott 2022)

Protests and lobbying eventually resulted in the three major networks of the 1970s agreeing in 1975 to avoid stereotypes of gay characters (Caputso 2013). Immediately, more and better LGBT+ characters (still white, gay men primarily) began to emerge. Although this was not wholly true, it did create a new age of representation that finally allowed gay characters to be more than just a one-time narrative for drama or a monster to slay. One of the first main characters who identified as homosexual was in 1977 in the show *Soap*. The character was Jodie Dallas, played by Billy Crystal. Although highly stereotypical by today's standards, some argue that the actor's embracement of the character and the fact that the character was allowed at all still make it a vital representation (Belonsky 2013).

The 1980s brought a rollercoaster of representation of LGBT+ characters in the United States. With a more conservative turn to politics, as well as the AIDS crisis causing panic, networks once again turned away from LGBT+ characters. However, the AIDS crisis brought structure to the LGBT+ community. Significant groups like the Gay and Lesbian Alliance Against Defamation (GLAAD) came into existence. They would change the landscape as gay rights now had large organizations that had gotten national attention thanks to the crisis. With the AIDS movement still fresh in the American mind, representation began to change. This change is not surprising when reviewing the representation of other minority groups. Clark (1969) discusses how, at the time, Black Americans were initially portrayed in a comedic light, but after the events of the Civil Rights Movement, more dramatic roles emerged that upheld 'law and order,' primarily civic roles in government (Clark 1969, 18-22).

The 1990s brought about a boom in representation. Many large movies, such as *Philadelphia* (1993) and *The Birdcage* (1996), were successful, and, as before, television followed. Kagan states,

> T.V. was even more prolific than Hollywood in its manufacturing of sexually unthreatening gay male characters. The secondary but permanent gay character became a staple of 1990s dramas and situation comedies, including NYPD Blue, Chicago, Hope, ER, Mad About You, and Roseanne. Eventually, queer protagonists became central characters in, for example, Ellen (1994–1998) and Dawson's Creek (1998–2003) (Kagan 2018).

Despite significant increases and upgrades in representation, there was little diversity among representation. The *GLAAD Where We Are On TV Report of 2022-2023* found that 35% of LGBT+ characters were gay, with lesbians slightly behind that at 30% and all other sexual orientations much lower than that (Deerwater 2023). The most significant change between the 1990s and now is that there has been an increase in racial diversity of LGBT+ characters, which is extremely important. In the 2022-2023 report, GLAAD found that 309 out of 596 LGBT+ characters were people of color. Compared to the 2007 report, where over seventy percent of LGBT+ characters were white, it is essential to progress (GLAADb n.d.). However, more work is needed. Given the limited transgender and ace representation available, many areas for improvement become clear.

Trans Representation

Transgender representation has grown in the past decade, but there are still significant areas that require improvement. In addition, the transgender community has decades of damaging stereotyped representation to undo, which makes it more difficult, as many audiences are coming into the media with pre-established biases against the community. While all LGBT+ identities face stereotypes and preconceived notions, transgender fictitious stereotypes act as ammunition to attack trans individuals not only by politicians (Bradner et al. 2023), but even by others in the LGBT+ community (Lavietes 2019). The most infamous representation stereotypes of transgender individuals in media include the sexual predator, the victim, and the joke. Despite the stereotype of trans individuals depicted as sexual predators, trans women are much more likely to be victims of sexual violence (Dowd 2023), with women of color even more likely to experience violence (Ussher et al. 2022). Positive representation tries to create fully developed characters who happen to be trans. Positive and complex representation has been found to offer emerging adults possibilities for their future and space for discussion (McInroy and Craig 2017). There is a wide range of the most detrimental trans representations in media, varying from poorly written to damaging representations.

One of the most harmful representations of trans individuals asserts the idea of the trans predator, pushing the stereotype that leads to poor mental health in transgender individuals (Hughto et al. 2021). GLAAD cataloged ten years of trans representation in television and found that transgender characters were portrayed as villains in twenty-one percent of television episodes that featured trans individuals (GLAADa n.d.). Early representations from *Psycho* and *The Lady Was a Man* created a trend of murderous trans individuals who target women (Abbott 2022). From there, many shows featured characters disguised as women who had violent intentions. An example of the lasting stereotype of the criminal trans depiction is in *Ace Ventura: Pet Detective*. In the movie, the main villain is revealed to be a man who has transitioned to a woman. The reaction of everyone around is over-the-top disgust, and the character is quickly disposed of in shame (Osenlund 2014). The movie is from 1994 and shows how, even in the early 1990s, trans representation was not only lacking but damaging. *CSI* (2000-2016) featured an episode about a transgender serial killer who mocked transgender victims in the show (GLAADa n.d.). This practice has become less common in the media, but it is not gone completely.

Other destructive representations paint trans individuals as victims of violence. GLAAD reported that forty percent of the time, trans individuals were depicted as victims (GLAADa n.d.). *Girl* (2018), a Netflix film, has been criticized as dangerous and harmful for its portrayal of a trans individual inflicting serious bodily harm on themselves (Piepenburg 2019). Dramas, in general, often use transgender identity as a plot device for drama or conflict, rather than exploring the genuine issues and experiences faced by transgender individuals. With transgender individuals already experiencing higher levels of violence than cisgender individuals in the real world (Dowd 2021), these fictitious depictions are damaging.

Using transgender individuals as the punchline for a joke is also a common trope. Shows such as *Family Guy* and *South Park* feature episodes where individuals are trans, and that is the joke. *Family Guy* has been using transgender individuals as the punchline for decades and shows no sign of stopping. In 2019, in the episode *Bri-Da*, the recurring character Ida is featured, and many jokes are made about the character's identity and promote the idea that trans individuals are 'privileged' in today's society (Rude 2019). *South Park* also had an episode in 2019, *Board Girls*, which mocked the ongoing discussion and issues around transgender athletes (Placido 2019). While the trend of using transgender individuals as a joke has died down, much like the previous conventionality, it has not gone away.

Conversely, some of the most positive transgender characters have come from the past few decades, although sadly, few are main characters. *Orange is the New Black* character Sophia Burset is one of the most famous examples from the 2010s. Sophia is a side character in the series whose journey goes through transphobia, racism, and many other fundamental issues that black trans individuals face. Sophia herself is an admirable character who is incredibly likable and fun to watch, as well as portrayed by an actual trans individual. The character is complex, and while her identity is part of her story, it is not her personality. However, the show and the portrayal are not without criticism. From a continuous barrage of struggles and discrimination (Allen, 2017) to the portrayal of Sophia's identity as a Black trans woman, the representation often falls short in addressing the complexities of her experience. (Thomas 2021). Intersectionality is critical within representation, especially with trans characters, as some of the founders of the LGBT+ rights movement were trans women of color, one of the groups that is not only underrepresented but experiences violence at a higher rate (Krell 2017) and even faces discrimination from the LGBT+ community (TranHub 2023). Despite the flaws, Sophia Burset was a character with a broad reach.

An interesting case is the show *The L Word* and the later follow-up, *The L Word: Generation Q*. The original show premiered in 2004 and faced significant criticism for how it portrayed trans character Max Sweeney. The journey the character was put through was dark and traumatic, portraying gender transitioning as a harrowing experience (Bendix 2019). The new series, *The L Word: Generation Q*, premiered in 2019, and two trans men of color and a trans woman portray a cisgender woman. Other positive portrayals include *The Chilling Adventures of Sabrina*, Theo Putnam, and *The Umbrella Academy* character Vanya Hargreeves. In a completely different category, the show *Pose* has arguably set a new standard for LGBT+ representation. Most of the lead characters are transgender, and they are also women of color. The show takes place during the 1980s and 1990s, a challenging time for the LGBT+ community with the AIDS crisis as well as political issues circulating. Abraham notes,

> Since 2002, GLAAD has kept track of trans representation in the media. After ten years, the organization found that 54 percent of shows featuring trans characters portrayed them negatively. Another 35 percent ranged from "problematic" to "good," and only 12 percent were considered groundbreaking (Abraham 2021).

Pose (2018-2021) is among that twelve percent. The show received five Emmy nominations in 2020 and over a million viewers (Goldberg 2023). Willis explains, despite this, queer and trans narratives especially those of people of color are still so often eclipsed by or laden with tragedy. Pose doesn't shy away from the hardships, but elevates the celebration and fellowship of these groups to the same level of importance (Willis 2018). While the show did not renew past a third season, viewers fondly remember it and have shown Hollywood that good representation can be just as, if not more lucrative, than the lazy and harmful tropes used in the past.

Authentic and complex transgender representation is becoming more common than in the past, but there is a much longer history of stereotypical, damaging representation. Depicting trans individuals as predators or only as victims of violence feeds into real-world problems and is detrimental to trans individuals' mental health. In addition, comedies that rely on the old trope of mocking the existence of transgender identity but defend it as 'satire' are continuing to feed into the problem. Positive representation is found in well-rounded characters who have a personality outside of their gender identity and have hardships and celebrations in life, as all humans do, not just tragedy. As good representation becomes more common and shows it can be successful, hopefully, writers will continue to make improvements rather than regress.

Asexual Representation

One of the biggest challenges in asexual representation is the sheer lack of visibility. GLAAD reported that no new characters identifying as asexual were introduced (Deerwater 2023). Because of this, comparisons of characters who are asexually coded or have a lack of sexual interest will also be included. Asexuals face the opposite issue of the trans community; instead of being oversexualized, asexuals face dehumanization due to a lack of sexual interest. Without acknowledging that not all asexuals are sex-repulsed, the other issue with this representation is how it 'others' the characters, treating them either as inhuman or as broken beings needing fixing.

The show *Sirens* (2018-2020) featured an asexual character, Valentina "Voodoo" Dunacci, whose sexuality becomes something for her and potential love interests to 'overcome,' a common trope associated with non-sexual characters. Another example of 'fixing' a character comes from the episode of *House* in the *Better Half,* where a husband's lack of sexual interest is at first attributed to asexuality, then turned into a medical diagnosis that needs treatment. While sexual dysfunction can be a symptom of medical issues, it is the main character's attitude throughout the episode that asexuality is 'fake' that makes the episode painful to watch. Overall, there are fewer than ten examples of asexual representation in the United States media. The lack of representation is not surprising, as asexuality has only been well-defined since the 1990s. However, other tropes surrounding a lack of sexual interest are still common in media and are harmful to asexual identities. A couple of those tropes include aliens and robots. Especially under the narrative of 'becoming human,' which almost always equates to sexual or romantic interest.

The most compelling asexual characters are well-rounded individuals whose identity is just one aspect of who they are, rather than defining their entire character or influencing how they react to every situation. One of the more detailed character arcs is from *Bojack Horseman*, the character Todd Chavez. Todd goes through the process of discovering his asexuality, goes through the process of dating, and finds community with others facing similar struggles. Todd Chavez does have criticism against his character, as do the other asexual characters in the show (Fijman 2023). The argument that Todd is 'naïve' and 'childlike,' which is a cliché of individuals not interested in sex, is interesting when juxtaposed with the idea that his potential love interest, Yolanda, is problematic for being defined by her sexuality. The lack of representation that the asexual community faces means that characters are expected to be every type of asexual. Not all asexuals have sexual repulsion; some are just less sexually active than others, rather than entirely non-sexual. There are few, if any, representations that show the vast diversity of the asexual spectrum. Another example would be aromantic, someone who does not experience romantic attraction.

Other representations include *the Game of Thrones* character Lord Varys, who was depicted as asexual but not due to the character being a eunuch. Lord Vary's asexuality pre-dates his eunuch status. In another show, *Everything is Going to be Okay* (2020-2021), the character Drea is asexual. The character goes through an arc with a female love interest and is autistic. There could be an argument that Drea is one of the main characters of her series, but Lord Varys is not. Another issue with asexual representation is that writers seem unable to maintain a story without the crutch of sex or romance, and thus avoid asexual characters as the center of a show.

Unlike transgender representation, asexual representation has a shorter history when tied to sexuality. Looking at how the media has reacted to the ideas of sexless or romanceless beings indicates potentially negative attitudes toward people on the asexual spectrum. The idea that a lack of sexual or romantic interest is something that inherently needs to be fixed is incredibly damaging to the asexual community and needs to be challenged. Especially since the media often ties the concept of 'love' to sexual attraction, rather than focusing on diverse, defined relationships. Asexuals are not less human for not feeling sexual attraction, and a more authentic, diverse representation could show the untold experiences of asexuals in a highly sexual world.

Improvements

Several improvements can be made to the current representation, but two areas of improvement would create the most progress. Diversity among creators is essential, and writing is still a predominantly white field. While representation between men and women is about equal, BIPOC women and men are underrepresented, especially in development and screenwriters (Writers Guild of America West 2022). More diversity needs to be seen at the development and screenwriting levels to create a more authentic representation that does not rely on stereotypes and broad generalizations that lead to shallow trans and asexual characters. At the very least, writers must consult with the individuals they represent. Even a white trans woman will not understand the experience of a Black trans woman and should not make assumptions about someone else's identity.

Having every LGBT+ person be white is a poor reflection of real life and limits stories in media. Diverse representations of LGBT+ characters challenge stereotypes and allow more individuals to see themselves represented. Diversity is not limited to race but also includes LGBT+ identities. So far, every asexual representation has just been asexual instead of an aromantic individual or demisexual. As stated above, diversity among writers is ideal, such as having an aromantic writer write an aromantic story, for example, but at the least, consultants are essential for accuracy and to avoid stereotypes.

Challenges and Advantages

Social perceptions and history of representation built the house's foundation, and there is no tearing it down overnight. Past representations raised the previous generation, influencing the culture of the United States toward LGBT+ communities. The biases of the past follow society into the present, and the only way to leave them behind is to create change. The LGBT+ community has seen tremendous changes not only in the United States but across the globe as well, but also a recession in areas that were once considered progressive. As the United States becomes more politically divided, marginal groups are used as scapegoats to further political agendas. In 2023 alone, there were over 400 bills against LGBT+ rights within the United States (American Civil Liberties Union 2023). While this trend may not continue, as public opinion is generally in favor of LGBT+ rights (Gallup Historical Trends 2023), damage from these bills and politicians' fear-mongering will last in parts of the country for decades to come.

One potential advantage is the rise of streaming platforms over traditional television and cable. According to a GLAAD report, streaming services featured 239 LGBT+ characters, compared to just 86 on primetime cable (Deerwater, 2023). This suggests that the more niche, siloed nature of streaming may be creating space for greater diversity in representation. Another promising development is the growing number of individuals identifying as LGBT+, now exceeding seven percent of the population (Jones, 2023).

Conclusion

The transgender community faces violence, over-sexualization, and mocking in much of the representation that has come out in the past. However, there are signs of improvement in modern representation, and the creation and circulation of damaging ideas cannot be undone overnight. On the other hand, asexual representation is so uncommon that the few representations that exist show a lack of understanding of what being asexual is really like. While the history of the representation is much shorter than the transgender identity, the idea of the non-sexual being that is inhuman has been around for decades and often casts a shadow on asexual representation. Both asexual and trans identities need more authentic representation in the media. Trans and asexual writers, actors, and writing consultants can help steer writers away from harmful tropes and create multifaceted characters. Better representations will influence the culture of the United States and move the media away from stereotypes and lazy writing.

References

Abbott, Traci. "TV and Films Have Long Taught Audiences Transphobia - The Washington Post." The Washington Post, July 14, 2022. https://www.washingtonpost.com/made-by-history/2022/07/14/tv-films-have-long-taught-audiences-transphobia/

Abraham, Mya. "Pose Set a New Standard For LGBTQ+ Representation on TV | POPSUGAR Entertainment." *Popsugar*, October 1, 2021. https://www.popsugar.com/entertainment/pose-set-new-standard-for-lgbtq-representation-on-tv-48532182

Acosta-Alzuru, Carolina. "'I'm Not a Feminist...I Only Defend Women as Human Beings': The Production, Representation, and Consumption of Feminism in a Telenovela." *Critical Studies in Media Communication* 20, no. 3 (September 2003): 269–94. https://doi.org/10.1080/07393180302775

Allen, Samantha. "Why Can't 'Orange Is the New Black' Stop Torturing Its Transgender Character?" *Daily Beast*, April 13, 2017. https://www.thedailybeast.com/why-cant-orange-is-the-new-black-stop-torturing-its-transgender-character

Appel, Markus, and Silvana Weber. "Do Mass Mediated Stereotypes Harm Members of Negatively Stereotyped Groups? A Meta-Analytical Review on Media-Generated Stereotype Threat and Stereotype Lift." *Communication Research* 48, no. 2 (March 2021): 151–79. https://doi.org/10.1177/00936502 17715543

Belonsky, Andrew. "Today in Gay History: Billy Crystal Goes Gay, Proudly." *Out*, September 13, 2013. https://www.out.com/entertainment/today-gay-history /2013/09/13/today-gay-history-billy-crystal-goes-gay-proudly

Bendix, Trish. "New 'The L Word: Generation Q' Wants to Do Right by Trans Men - Los Angeles Times." *Los Angeles Times*, November 26, 2019. https://www. latimes.com/entertainment-arts/tv/story/2019-11-26/glaad-trans-represen tation-the-l-word-generation-q-showtime

Berry, Gordon. "Television and Afro-Americans: Past Legacy and Present Portrayls." In *Television and Social Behavior : Beyond Violence and Children / a Report of the Committee on Television and Social Behavior, Social Science Research Council*, 231–48, 1980. https://ebookcentral.proquest.com/lib/grin nell-ebooks/reader.action?pq-origsite=primo&ppg=246&docID=1323339

Bradner, Eric, Steve Contorno, and Kate Sullivan. "Republicans Ramp up Attacks on Transgender People, in Statehouses and on the Campaign Trail | CNN Politics." *CNN*, April 30, 2023. https://www.cnn.com/2023/04/30/ politics/republicans-transgender-attacks-statehouse-haley-trump/index.html

Capsuto, Steven. *Alternate Channels : The Uncensored Story of Gay and Lesbian Images on Radio and Television*. New York: Ballantine Books, 2000. https:// archive.org/details/alternatechannel00stev/mode/2up

Castro, Juanjo Bermudez De. "Psycho Killers, Circus Freaks, Ordinary People: A Brief History of the Representation of Transgender Identities on American TV Series," 2017.

Clark, Cedric. "Television and Social Control: Some Observations on the Portrayals of Ethnic Minorities." *Television Quarterly* 8 (1969): 18–22. https:// doi.org/10.1525/fq.1969.22.3.04a00050

Deerwater, Raina. "GLAAD's 27th Annual Where We Are on TV Report Sees Growing Racial Diversity among LGBTQ Characters, Overall LGBTQ Representation Slightly Down | GLAAD." GLAAD, March 17, 2023. https:// glaad.org/glaads-27th-annual-where-we-are-tv-report-sees-growing-racial- diversity-among-lgbtq-characters/

Di Placido, Dani. "'South Park' Review: 'Board Girls' Touches A Divisive Topic With Kid Gloves." Forbes, November 14, 2019. https://www.forbes.com/ sites/danidiplacido/2019/11/14/south-park-review-board-girls-touches-a- divisive-topic-with-kid-gloves/?sh=5d581cd3681f

Dowd, Rebecca. "Transgender People over Four Times More Likely than Cisgender People to Be Victims of Violent Crime - Williams Institute." UCLA School of Law Williams Institute. Accessed September 12, 2023. https:// williamsinstitute.law.ucla.edu/press/ncvs-trans-press-release/

Fijman, Sophia. "Misguided Monoliths: BoJack Horseman and the Reality of Asexuality — Spotlight." Spotlight, May 2, 2023. https://www.spotlight journal.org/issue-iii/c8wrpyaklih2spq3xqebzij6qd8c2s

GLAADa. n.d.. "Victims or Villains: Examining Ten Years of Transgender Images on Television | GLAAD." Accessed September 12, 2023. https://glaad.org/ publications/victims-or-villains-examining-ten-years-transgender-images- television/

GLAADb. n.d.. "Where We Are on TV Report: 2007 – 2008 Season." Accessed September 7, 2023. https://glaad.org/publications/tvreport08/

Goldberg, Leslie. "'Pose' Scores Early Season 3 Renewal at FX – The Hollywood Reporter." The Hollywood Reporter. Accessed September 12, 2023. https://www.hollywoodreporter.com/tv/tv-news/pose-scores-early-season-3-renewal-at-fx-1218982/

Goodwill, Janelle R., Nkemka Anyiwo, Ed-Dee G. Williams, Natasha C. Johnson, Jacqueline S. Mattis, and Daphne C. Watkins. "Media Representations of Popular Culture Figures and the Construction of Black Masculinities." *Psychology of Men & Masculinities* 20, no. 3 (July 2019): 288–98. https://doi.org/10.1037/men0000164

Hall, Stuart. *Representation : Cultural Representations and Signifying Practices.* Sage in association with the Open University, 1997.

Hughto, Jaclyn M.W., David Pletta, Lily Gordon, Sean Cahill, Matthew J. Mimiaga, and Sari L. Reisner. "Negative Transgender-Related Media Messages Are Associated with Adverse Mental Health Outcomes in a Multistate Study of Transgender Adults." *LGBT Health* 8, no. 1 (January 1, 2021): 32–41. https://doi.org/10.1089/lgbt.2020.0279

"Inclusion & Equity Report 2022." Writers Guild of America West, 2022. https://deadline.com/wp-content/uploads/2022/04/inclusion-report-2022.pdf.

Jones, Jeffrey. "U.S. LGBT Identification Steady at 7.2%." Gallup. Accessed September 12, 2023. https://news.gallup.com/poll/470708/lgbt-identification-steady.aspx.

Kagan, Dion. *Positive Images : Gay Men and HIV/AIDS in the Culture of "Post Crisis."* London: I. B. Tauris & Company, Limited, 2018.

Krell, Elías Cosenza. "Is Transmisogyny Killing Trans Women of Color?" *TSQ: Transgender Studies Quarterly* 4, no. 2 (May 1, 2017): 226–42. https://doi.org/10.1215/23289252-3815033

Lavietes, Matthew. "Tensions between Trans Women and Gay Men Boil over at Stonewall Anniversary | Reuters." Thomson Reuters, June 28, 2019. https://www.reuters.com/article/us-gay-pride-transgender/tensions-between-trans-women-and-gay-men-boil-over-at-stonewall-anniversary-idUSKCN1TV0V0

"LGBTQ+ Rights | Gallup Historical Trends." Accessed September 8, 2023. https://news.gallup.com/poll/1651/gay-lesbian-rights.aspx

"Mapping Attacks on LGBTQ Rights in U.S. State Legislatures | American Civil Liberties Union." Accessed December 7, 2023. https://www.aclu.org/legislative-attacks-on-lgbtq-rights

McInroy, Lauren B., and Shelley L. Craig. "Perspectives of LGBTQ Emerging Adults on the Depiction and Impact of LGBTQ Media Representation." *Journal of Youth Studies* 20, no. 1 (January 2, 2017): 32–46. https://doi.org/10.1080/13676261.2016.1184243

Moylan, Brian. "Most LGBT Characters on US TV Are White and Male, Study Finds | US Television | The Guardian." The Guardian, November 27, 2015. https://www.theguardian.com/tv-and-radio/2015/oct/27/most-lgbt-characters-on-us-tv-are-white-and-male-study-finds

Osenlund, R. Kurt. "Sinful Cinema: Ace Ventura: Pet Detective, The Most Offensive Football Movie Ever Made - Slant Magazine." Slant, January 31, 2014. https://www.slantmagazine.com/film/sinful-cinema-ace-ventura-pet-detective-the-most-offensive-and-homophobic-football-movie-ever-made/

Piepenburg, Erik. "Is a Film About a Transgender Dancer Too 'Dangerous' to Watch? - The New York Times." New York Times, January 2, 2019. https://www.nytimes.com/2019/01/02/movies/girl-netflix-film-transgender-debate.html

Rosen, Rebecca. "A Glimpse Into 1970s Gay Activism - The Atlantic." The Atlantic, February 26,2014. https://www.theatlantic.com/politics/archive/2014/02/a-glimpse-into-1970s-gay-activism/284077/

Rude, Mey. "'Family Guy' Is Still Just as Transphobic as Ever." Out, October 7, 2019. https://www.out.com/television/2019/10/07/family-guy-still-just-transphobic-ever

Thomas, Victoria E. "Gazing at 'It': An Intersectional Analysis of Transnormativity and Black Womanhood in Orange Is the New Black." Communication, Culture and Critique 13, no. 4 (January 26, 2021): 519–35. https://doi.org/10.1093/ccc/tcz030

TransHub. "Why Are Trans People Part of LGBT? — TransHub." Accessed September 11, 2023. https://www.transhub.org.au/101/trans-lgbt

Ussher, Jane M., Alexandra Hawkey, Janette Perz, Pranee Liamputtong, Jessica Sekar, Brahmaputra Marjadi, Virginia Schmied, Tinashe Dune, and Eloise Brook. "Crossing Boundaries and Fetishization: Experiences of Sexual Violence for Trans Women of Color." Journal of Interpersonal Violence 37, no. 5–6 (March 2022): NP3552–84. https://doi.org/10.1177/0886260520949149

Willis, Raquel. "'Pose' Is the TV Series Queer and Trans People of Color Deserve | Them." Them, June 3, 2018. https://www.them.us/story/pose-fx-qtpoc-representation

Chapter Seven
The Monstrous Rainbow Swastika: The Horror Genre's Queer Nazi versus Historical Fact

Abigail Waldron
Horror Press LLC

Abstract

The horror genre has a history of perpetuating dangerous stereotypes that have existed in Hollywood since the 1940s that revolve around queer Nazism. The history of Nazi persecution of queer folks, particularly gay men and trans individuals, is often overlooked when discussing the Holocaust. As a result, films in search of titillating shock value, many of which are horror films, revert back to these malicious stereotypes when writing queer characters. Particularly, I focus on *The Silence of the Lambs'* Buffalo Bill (1991) and Ms. Mann from the Wayans Brothers' *Scary Movie* (2000), two very popular horror movies that have used queer characters as conduits for Nazism. Without proper education on Nazi persecution of queer folks in the Holocaust, Hollywood continues to equate Nazism with queerness, despite the overwhelming amount of historical facts that contradict, or at the very least, distort this history. Horror films, meant to scare and shock, use the myth of queer Nazis to frighten audiences without acknowledging the dangerous problem of Holocaust-misinformation.

Through this piece, the chapter dives into the history of queer persecution by the Third Reich. Importantly, I discuss Ernst Rohm, an openly gay Nazi and leader of Hitler's earlier iteration of the SS, and how his legacy helped to shape the misconceptions of queerness within Nazi ranks. The study also goes into the invaluable research conducted by Dr. Magnus Hirschfeld, whose research of queer folks, especially intersex and transgender, was groundbreaking and, unfortunately, destroyed by fascist youths in the mid-1930s. This history directly correlates to how Hollywood treats queer villains. Nazis have been queered by Hollywood since the 1930s in an effort to discredit the Third Reich and further prove their 'perversion.'

The lack of understanding of queer persecution in the Holocaust has had two notable effects of which this piece concerns: 1) Hollywood, especially films of salacious genres such as horror, have used Nazism to make queer characters more frightening and predatory, and 2) as a result, the mythic queer Nazi has infiltrated popular culture with these outrageous characters, and this further alienated audiences from the facts of the Holocaust.

Keywords: Horror, History, Nazi, Holocaust

***

Introduction

Be it the countless American school boards banning books or anti-mask protesters during the COVID-19 pandemic, ignorance toward the Holocaust persists in the American consciousness. (Kasakove, 2022; Samberg et al., 2021). Several studies from the past few years show that time and time again, misconceptions about the Holocaust are pervasive worldwide. The ignorance on display concerns arguments regarding whether the Holocaust was about race, if children should be educated on the subject, and if being required to wear a mask to help prevent the spread of COVID-19 is equivalent to Jewish people in Europe being forced to wear a yellow star under Nazi rule. Our general misunderstanding about one of the most gruesome events in world history is not new. Since 1945, the Holocaust has become clouded by misinterpretations and outright hatred toward the targets of the genocide through Holocaust denial efforts as well as media representations (even well-meaning ones; SPLC, 2023). Additionally, some victims of the Holocaust have been relegated to the sidelines of history, particularly queer folks. This demographic is oft-forgotten, ripe for misinterpretations to be conjured and spun into subconscious fact. Unfortunately, films, particularly horror films, are partly to blame for the mass un-remembering of queer Holocaust victims and survivors, and aid in the mythical correlation between queerness and Nazism.

Films about Nazis and the Holocaust are linked to horror – retellings and interpretations of true horrific and unfathomable events are not bound to genre constraints. The one aspect holding historical Holocaust films back from being labeled 'horror' is the omission of the fantastic, which almost always accompanies horror films. Stories of the Holocaust are terrifying, often unimaginable to audiences who have never lived through such a reality. Unfortunately, some horror films exploit Nazi and Holocaust imagery and use real horrors as inspiration with little regard for historical fact. These exploitations have perpetuated misconceptions about the Holocaust, its victims, and survivors. For the sake of scaring audiences with Nazi imagery, the horror films in question have helped to erase the experiences of Holocaust victims and survivors, particularly LGBTQ+ individuals.

Using Nazi and Holocaust imagery, horror films perpetuate false narratives of the Holocaust, erasing survivor testimony in favor of caricatures of queer Nazis. Films such as Oscar-winner *The Silence of the Lambs* (1991) and horror-comedy *Scary Movie* (2000) use Nazi imagery as a means to villainize queer characters, effectively perpetuating the notion that queer people, especially transgender people and gay men, weren't victims of the Holocaust, but rather, accomplices. *The Damned* (1969), for instance, begins in 1933 with a drag performance by Martin, the son of a Nazi-sympathizing businessman. The film's poster shows Martin, in drag, with a tagline that ominously reads "He was soon to become the second most powerful man in Nazi Germany." He becomes the embodiment of perversion and depravity throughout the film. *The Damned* also includes scenes depicting The Night of the Long Knives, though the US release of the film cut nearly all of these sequences (Visconti, 1969). Films like *The Damned* (1969) and *Apt Pupil* (1998) use literal queer Nazis, whose sexualities are synonymous with their fascist identities and ideology, as antagonists. In this piece, I will give a history of queer persecution in Nazi Germany, the historic queer realities of both victims and perpetrators of Nazi violence, and how horror has actively exploited Nazi terror to perpetuate harmful stereotypes of queer people, effectively silencing and erasing gay survivors of the Holocaust.

Homosexual Persecution, Feminization, and Murder Under Nazi Rule

Before the rise of Nazism, Berlin, Germany was a hub for queer activity. It was here that Dr. Magnus Hirschfeld, a prominent gay Jewish physician and sexologist, established the *Institut für Sexualwissenschaft* in 1919 to document queer and trans life and advocate for their rights. After fourteen years of collecting invaluable work for the gay rights movement, on May 6, 1933, a group of youths from the burgeoning Nazi movement ransacked the institute, its vast and irreplaceable archives of material burned.

Homosexuality had been deemed an enemy of the German people by Nazi propagandists, claiming Germany could not be at full strength with homosexuals in its populace. In a published statement in May of 1928, the Nazi Party made clear their stance: "Anyone who thinks of homosexual love is our enemy. We reject anything which emasculates our people and makes it a plaything for our enemies..." (Plant 1988, 50). Paragraph 175, an 1871 law criminalizing homosexuality among men which was almost eradicated from German legislature thanks to the efforts of individuals like Dr. Hirschfeld, was solidified under Hitler's reign in 1935. The official Hitler newspaper years earlier accurately predicted the strengthening of Paragraph 175 in a rebuttal to Dr. Hirschfeld's activism: "National Socialists will soon unmask and condemn [homosexuality] by law... we will punish [homosexuals] by banishment or hanging" (Plant 1988, 49).

According to the Holocaust Memorial Day Trust, an estimated 10-15,000 men were sent to concentration camps for being homosexual (HMDT, 2023). This number doesn't include the countless queer women, as well as transgender and intersex folks, who were also subjected to incarceration and unimaginable torture by the Nazis. These inmates were either branded "homosexual" and given the designation of the pink triangle, or designated as "asocial" and given the black triangle alongside prostitutes, the mentally handicapped, and drug addicts.

Richard Plant, in his groundbreaking book *The Pink Triangle: The Nazi War Against Homosexuals* (1986), explains that historians have a record of feminizing Nazis to make them even more threatening. This is the case with the long-standing discourse over Hitler's sexual preferences, including the possibility of being queer himself. In 2010, Bryan Fischer of The American Family Association, an anti-gay lobby, asserted that "Homosexuality gave us Adolf Hitler, and homosexuality in the military gave us the Brown Shirts, the Nazi war machine and six million dead Jews" (SPLC, 2022). This tactic of queering Hitler and Nazis effectively attempts to make their malevolence more sinister: "The technique of homosexualizing the enemy [...] can be understood as a thirst for revenge, but it does not excuse such gleeful illogic – they simultaneously depict Hitler as wickedly effeminate but stop short of proving that he was homosexual. What they did was to indict him by association" (Plant 1988, 15). As contradictory as it seems, Hitler's early rise to power would not have been possible without Ernst Röhm, the openly gay chief of the *Sturmabteilung* (SA) and Hitler's right-hand man in the Third Reich from 1919 to 1934.

Nazis were aware of Röhm's sexuality, even Hitler. He and his SA, known as the Brown Shirts, which grew from 300,000 to 3 million members from 1933 to 1934, began raiding gay bars in Germany in 1933 following a Nazi decree banning gathering places for homosexuals. Röhm was a passionate military man, devoted to the notion that Germany's problems would be solved with a technological monarchy. He became a close confidant of Hitler during his early rise, despite his well-acknowledged homosexuality. Röhm's organizational skills were not only admirable to Hitler but useful – his homosexuality was largely ignored by the Führer (Plant 1988, 59). He would later go on to say, after more complaints about Röhm's homosexuality, "His private life cannot be an object of scrutiny unless it conflicts with basic principles of National Socialist ideology" (Plant 1988, 61). Both Röhm's military ambitions and his homosexuality would be the reasons for his eventual execution.

Röhm, who wanted to be a soldier since childhood, in no way fit the mold of the effeminate homosexual as asserted by Nazi propaganda. He enjoyed training rugged Nazi pupils and rose in the ranks within the Nazi Party. The only complaints about him concerned his abrasiveness and contempt for his superiors. It was these complaints and the resulting animosity from high-ranking Nazi officials that led to his death. In 1934, during the Night of the Long Knives, Hitler, spurred by paranoia that Röhm and other SA officials were planning a coup to replace Germany's army with the unruly SA, ordered mass arrests of SA officers. Hundreds of these "extremists" were killed to appease Hitler's moderate supporters, who would help catapult him to the Führer. Hitler called them "homosexual pigs," though he was aware that not all SA men were gay (Plant 1988, 56). Röhm was executed on July 1st. In typical Hitler fashion, despite his years-long relationship with Röhm, he used Röhm's homosexuality as a scapegoat for his execution, despite his sexuality being a non-issue for years. "[Röhm's] unapologetic behavior," explains Plant, "had provided a convenient peg on which Hitler could hang a multitude of sins... Homosexuality within the SA was used by Hitler as a ploy so that he could pose as the moral leader..." (Plant 1988, 67). The Night of the Long Knives, the first permissible act of wholesale murder by the state, along with the obsession of homosexual eradication by Hitler's head of the SS, Heinrich Himmler, would be the roots of the future calculated genocide of several marginalized groups. It began with the murder of a gay Nazi. Like Röhm, the British far-right personality and provocateur Milo Yiannopoulos openly embraced his homosexuality in connection with his conservative beliefs. Yiannapoulos disregarded the reality of queer folks during the Holocaust and chose to align himself with his oppressor, opting for aesthetics (used heavily in Nazisploitation films) rather than objective truths about Nazism.

Two years after the execution of Röhm and the dissolution of the SA, Heinrich Himmler, the prudish yet menacing devotee of the Nazi Party, was appointed chief of the SS and established the Federal Security Office for Combatting Abortion and Homosexuality. Among the many homophobic sentiments he had since adolescence, Himmler believed homosexuals to be useless members of German society – they could not procreate and birth Aryans. He also believed gay men were cowards, effeminate, and could not fight. There is little doubt that Himmler's hatred of Ernst Röhm is charged with envy. Röhm was an accomplished gay soldier, while Himmler struggled with physicality and sports all his life. "[L]ike stinging nettles," Himmler asserts, "we will rip [homosexuals] out, throw them on a heap, and burn them" (Plant 1988, 89).

Although gay men were the minority among other groups sent to camps across Europe, they received some of the hardest work details. Additionally, they suffered from a lack of access to any position of power among the ranks of prisoners due to the varying economic and social backgrounds of the gay prisoners. Rape, forced prostitution, extreme humiliation, torturous medical experiments with hormones and castration, mind-numbing and often meaningless hard labor, and abuse from other prisoners dominated the lives of homosexual men in the camps, resulting in alienation and dehumanization. Unlike the typical block, designated queer blocks, such as in Flossenburg and Sachsenhausen, were heavily monitored for sexual activity, with lights being kept on at night and strict rules to keep hands and arms above the covers under threat of beating or death (Heger 1980, 47-48). Predatory guards took advantage of the alienated homosexual men by performing sex acts on or near them. In many cases, as a means of protection or food rations due to desperation, homosexual prisoners were essentially coerced or forced to offer themselves to the guards (Plant 1988, 167). Heinz Heger, a detained homosexual inmate at Sachsenhausen, documents in *The Men with the Pink Triangle* not only the brutality inflicted upon gay men but the double standards and homophobia they endured among their fellow prisoners.

> The prisoners with the pink triangle were, as always, "filthy queers" [...] the very fellow-prisoners who insulted and condemned us... were unperturbed by [sexual] relationships that the block seniors and Capos had with the young Poles [...] And so the way a person was assessed by his fellows had two sides to it [...] Homosexual behavior between two "normal" men is considered an emergency outlet, while the same thing between two gay men, who both feel deeply for one another, is something "filthy" and repulsive. (Heger 1980, 61)

Another survivor of Sachsenhausen recalls his supervisor of a penal labor battalion referring to men with the pink triangle as "menwomen," a signifier of the historical false correlation between homosexuality and transgenderism that would be echoed in *The Silence of the Lambs* nearly fifty years later (Plant 1988, 171). Even before the end of the war, the torture endured by homosexual men was already being dismissed by their fellow prisoners. The historical erasure of gay suffering had begun in the camps and would continue for several decades.

Queer Nazis in Horror

Horror puts on display the societal misfit, monster, and outcast, making it the perfect genre for subtextual and outright queer discourse. Unfortunately, these roots are often tangled in misrepresentations, resulting in queer villain stereotypes. The use of queer Nazis in horror is not new. Before the United States entered World War II, Hollywood was prepared to have the ultimate on-screen villain, and from the onset, was more than willing to incorporate additional social and moral perversions. Luckily however, the Production Code, which gained more authority by 1934, put a stop to what would have been an early film depiction of a gender-bending Nazi. *The Black Cat* (1934), starring horror titans Bela Lugosi and Boris Karloff and directed by Jewish director

Edgar Ulmer, is a sadomasochistic tale of evil Satanists. According to historian Harry M. Benshoff in his foundational work *Monsters in the Closet: Homosexuality and the Horror Film* (1997), Ulmer's original vision was to depict the Satanists "as aberrant as possible" with the inclusion of Frau Goering (Benshoff 1998, 65). Goering would have been played by a male actor adorned with a dark, fuzzy mustache on her upper lip. Due to Goering's gender non-conforming, Code enforcers did not permit Ulmer to include her in the final cut. "Ulmer's resultant vision," asserts Benshoff, "would have succeeded in conflating homosexuality with Nazism, yet another monstrous signifier of same-sex desire which continues to circulate through popular culture" (Benshoff 1998, 65). In this rare case, the Production Code actually spared queer people from seeing such a character. The Code would eventually be replaced by the MPAA rating system in 1968.

When examining horror's use of Nazi aesthetics for queer, and especially trans, characters, there must be an acknowledgment of horror's mutant cinematic cousin: exploitation. In the decades after World War II, filmmakers, mostly European, attempted to portray the fascist era by creating their versions of Nazis through the medium of exploitation. This low-budget, sleazy action/thriller subgenre prioritizes gore, sexual fetish (particularly bondage and leather), and uses taboo subject matter to shock audiences. As suggested by the countless crude titles like *SS Experiment Love Camp* (1976), the genre was, at its core, ahistorical. Some directors claim to have heavily researched the Holocaust before filming, allegedly using their findings as inspiration for their onscreen atrocities. The depraved and perverted Nazis developed from those with a dangerous disregard for history dominated the genre

While some of these films attempted to add to the post-fascist discourse, the majority were purely designed to shock, be it through concentration camp torture scenes or explicit sexual favors for the Third Reich. This was not a new phenomenon, however. Beginning with the trial of Ilse Koch in 1947, media representations of the Holocaust, aided by legal and historical professionals, sexualized and fetishized Nazi abuse within the camps. The trial of Ilse Koch, wife of Buchenwald commandant Karl-Otto Koch, shocked and intrigued a public curious as to just what hideous acts "the Bitch of Buchenwald" committed. While the allegations about human skin lampshades have remained unproven, these and other sordid stories and witness testimony solidified her as a true Nazi monster. Her trial prosecutor even described her as "no woman in the usual sense but a creature from some other tortured world" (Simic 2023). The sexualization and monsterization of Koch were revamped less than thirty years later through Nazisploitation, further entrenching Nazi myths into popular culture.

In the documentary *Fascism On A Thread: The Strange Story of Nazisploitation Cinema* (2019), when examining the film *The Damned*, author John Martin explains the correlation in early post-WWII cinema between Nazism and homosexuality: "[T]o signify the descent into depravity [of the fictional family in *The Damned*]... homosexuality is often deemed to be a sign of Nazism... it's sort of questionable from today's perspective that these things will be linked as deplorable things" (Holwill 2019). Author Kim Newman extrapolates Martin's point in his analysis of the gratuitous, warped, and downright inappropriate *Ilsa: She Wolf of the SS* (1975), a film inspired by Ilse Koch. She explains that, despite the plain physical appearances of female SS officers including Koch, their respective films portrayed them as "...Playboy pinups in abbreviated, tailored, low-cut SS uniforms... something that actual Nazis would have horribly disapproved of." She adds, "However, maybe one of our revenges of history is associating Nazis with *all the things they hated*" (Holwill 2019).

Newman's observation is optimistic. While yes, many cinematic Nazis were satirically painted with traits that they would disagree with and are contrary to historical records, it is also true that filmmakers gave them traits that the larger American public found deplorable. In David Fernbach's 1980 introduction to Heger's *The Men with the Pink Triangle*, he surmises the problematic nature of these narratives conjured by supposed anti-fascist filmmakers, of which several claimed to have been in *Fascism on a Thread*. In reference to Röhm's high-ranking status within the Nazi regime while being openly gay, Fernbach asserts that it was these opportunist filmmakers who helped to perpetuate the misinformation and myth-making of the queer Nazi. "The left," he stressed in 1980, "had never gone beyond a 'sickness' theory of homosexuality [referring to the mentally-ill designation by medical professionals given to queer folks throughout the twentieth century], even in its support for legislation, and now had additional 'proof' of the sickness of fascism..." (Heger 1980, 11). Queers being painted with the "brush of fascism" persists beyond the twentieth century. Its effects can be seen in current far-right discourse and on the silver screen.

In horror and exploitation, while the public knows of Nazi war crimes, it is not enough to have a historically accurate Nazi on film. Horror opted for making the Nazis even more depraved and perverted, done in part by looking to American history and locating a group that has been viewed and treated as, among many things, demonic, sinful, a danger to children, and sexually disturbed. Films like *The Damned* and *Ilsa* paved the way for the queer Nazis of horror, specifically in the mainstream. This new interpretation insinuated that Nazis are inherently queer for the sake of depravity.

Unlike the international directors and writers of the exploitation genre, American filmmakers seldom touched the Holocaust unless equipped with adequate knowledge. This was not the case with American horror, which often used Nazis (queer or otherwise) as fright fodder. While *The Monster Squad* (1988) remains an example of how horror filmmakers can create a sympathetic portrayal of a Holocaust survivor, the breadth of horror cinema has used the trope of the queer Nazi, which further demonized queer folks (Dekker 1987). Two such films, both highly prevalent in popular culture, are the Wayans Brothers' *Scary Movie* (2000) and Jonathan Demme's *The Silence of the Lambs* (1991), based on the book by Thomas Harris. Sadly, the latter enlists the classic villainous Nazi trope of being gay and effeminate. Thanks to the centuries-long misconception and misunderstanding of what it means to be transgender, the evil of both these films' villains is their being Nazi-sympathizing transgender people.

The Silence of the Lambs' Buffalo Bill is one of the most iconic and well-known horror film villains in the history of film. He is not only a gay serial killer of women to make female skin suits, but he also claims to be transgender. This is later refuted by the cannibalistic psychologist Dr. Lecter in a conversation with FBI agent Clarice Starling:

> Clarice: "There's no correlation in the literature between transsexualism and violence…"

> Lecter: "Clever girl! […] Billy is not a real transsexual, but he thinks he is, […] Billy hates his own identity, you see, and he thinks that makes him a transsexual. But his pathology is a thousand times more savage and more terrifying." (Demme 1991)

His savage pathology can be seen not only in the physical sewing of female skin suits but also in scene backgrounds. As Bill rushes to grab his gun in the film's final climax, his bedspread is quickly revealed: a swastika-emblazoned quilt. Buffalo Bill is inspired by notorious American serial killer Ed Gein, among other murderers, who used the body parts of his victims for clothing and furniture (Biography, 2023). While Bill is inspired by Gein, it is more than possible that Gein himself had read of similar crimes of the Holocaust, including medical experimentation and of those alleged of the infamous Ilse Koch. Haley E. Solomon and Beth Kurtz-Costes, assisted by Dolf Zillman's exemplification theory, explain in their study "*Media's Influence on Perceptions of Trans Women*" (2018) that audiences' covert or open prejudices were enhanced and/or developed when viewing a provocative and negative portrayal of a transgender woman (Solomon & Kurtz-Costes, 2018). Bill's sadism and apparent fascist leanings, aided by his provocative and unforgettable dance sequence, assisted in viewers' correlation between his queerness and his embrace of Nazi ideology. In Netflix's documentary *Disclosure*, actress Jen Richards reveals that her friend immediately referred to Buffalo Bill when she came out to her as trans (Feder, 2020). *The Silence of the Lambs* won Best Film at the 1992 Oscars, forever solidifying Buffalo Bill's popular culture relevancy and altering cisgender perceptions of trans folks.

Though a much lighter film than *The Silence of the Lambs*, *Scary Movie* echoes the transphobic and homophobic sentiments of the Buffalo Bill character with their own transgender character, Miss Mann. Mann is a predatory gym teacher who transitioned "to gain the athletic edge on the competition" (Wayans, 2000). Not only does she make passes at the underage girls in the locker room, but she later brushes her testicles against protagonist Cindy's arm. Earlier in the scene, as Miss Mann, played by cisgender female bodybuilder Jayne Trcka, sniffs a pair of girls' underwear, an SS uniform is visibly hanging behind her on a coat rack. It is never mentioned or explained. This SS uniform was accompanied by mannequin hands in positions of sexual bondage, making it a clear example of the influence of Nazisploitation on popular cinema and perceptions of queer sexuality by heterosexual and cisgender writers. Like Buffalo Bill's swastika-covered quilt in a blink-and-you-miss-it scene, there seems to be no purpose to these inclusions other than to make these queer characters appear more perverted. It does not help that historians have uncovered hundreds of photos, collected by artist Martin Dammann, of on and off-duty Nazi soldiers cross-dressing, further skewing the public perception of Nazis as being not only inherently evil but inherently queer.

Being a Nazi in horror is not scary enough for Hollywood. This becomes clear with Bryan Singer's 1998 adaptation of acclaimed horror author Stephen King's novella "*Apt Pupil.*" Both the writer and director of the story, as explained in *Frames of Evil: The Holocaust as Horror in American Film*, "employ landscapes of misogyny and homophobia, respectively, to increase the stakes of evil in their monsters" (Picart and Frank 2006, 124). *Apt Pupil*, directed by Bryan Singer and starring Hollywood heavyweight and openly gay Ian McKellen as a former Nazi officer, had no issues with transferring the homoeroticism between Nazi war criminal Dussander (McKellen) and Todd (Brad Renfro) to the big screen. The film does not flinch when it comes to Nazi depravity and the fascination with abomination. "In this film," historians Picart and Frank explain, "evil has a face—Nazism, which is configured as quintessentially innate, supernaturally crafty, and in a more subterranean way, dangerously blurring of the boundaries between homoeroticism and homosexuality" (Picart and Frank 2006, 100). Additionally, the implication of pedophilia surrounds this film both on-screen and off: In 1997, Bryan Singer, openly bisexual, was accused of sexual misconduct in a deleted scene involving teenage boys/actors in a shared gym shower, furthering the mythic correlation between homosexuality and sexually assaulting children (Picart and Frank

2006, 116-117). Todd and Dussander's relationship throughout the film suggests that Todd is turning more queer with the prevalence of Dussander in his life. The more time they spend together, the more intertwined they become. Singer's film implies that Dussander is queering and effectively perverting Todd. The intermingling of Holocaust imagery with homoeroticism between a former Nazi SS officer and a teenage boy has frightening implications. Not only is Todd becoming more and more entrenched in Nazism, but to make matters worse as insinuated by Singer's film, he is becoming gay. Todd loses interest in girls, unless he imagines sadistic Holocaust rape scenarios much like the ones in Nazisploitation, and is focused on the old man living next door. Scenes with a solo Dussander involve sexual fantasies, one in which his masturbation in front of a mirror evokes Buffalo Bill in his memorable dance in front of a camera (Picart and Frank 2006, 118). Both are attracted to themselves as monsters, as Nazis. And unfortunately, their monstrosity is connected to their possible queerness.

A surprising subversion of the queer Nazi trope appeared in *Puppet Master: The Littlest Reich* (2018), written by Jewish screenwriter Steven Craig Zahler. Although the film adheres to exploitation fanfare, *The Littlest Reich* made clear its intentions to highlight the types of people the Nazis named deviant, and therefore disposable, without slipping into the queer Nazi stereotype in the process. In its opening scenes, the film includes a queer female couple who discuss their future together raising a family in 1986 Texas. Villain Nazi war criminal Toulon utters "disgusting homosexuals" in their direction and soon kills them with his murderous puppets (Laguna & Wiklund 2018). Lesbians, though their queerness was not illegal according to the Nazi creed, are often forgotten victims of the Holocaust. It was believed, however, that lesbians would be easily cured. Thus, they were not perceived as threats to the Aryan race as highly as homosexual men. Nevertheless, scores of lesbians were subjected to the same tortures as other "deviants" (Laguna & Wiklund 2018).

In America and abroad, we have become accustomed to seeing neo-Nazis and far-right homophobic and racist factions. Thanks in part to media representation, Americans tend to see these groups as fringe, and in some cases, benign, chalking up their behavior to idiocy and ignorance rather than their explicitly spiritually, philosophically, and physically violent ethos. This is extremely dangerous and suggests that we are forgetting the history and legacy of the Third Reich. "The ideological and social-structural implications of this formation are essentially problematic, for they rely on the same hetero-centric assumptions that give rise to fascist values, that is, the criminalization of individuals based on sexuality" (Picart and Frank 2006, 124). In 2023, we have seen a widespread embrace of homophobic and transphobic legislation, governance, and philosophy, with Florida being the most transparent in its efforts to demonize and criminalize queerness. What is most ominous is that many cisgender, heterosexual Americans are blind to this fascist rise, with few folks understanding or even being knowledgeable of the early stages of the Holocaust in 1930s Europe. It was the homosexuals, among other "asocials," who were the earliest targets for Nazis. It appears states like Florida are repeating history.

Acknowledging Queer Holocaust Survivors

Organizations such as the Conference on Jewish Material Claims Against Germany have been dedicated to compensating Holocaust survivors worldwide since the end of World War II. However, it was not until September 2021 that the German government reported on its initiative to provide additional compensation to survivors imprisoned for male homosexuality, after having endured decades of erasure, continued punishment, and shame. According to the German Federal Office of Justice in 2021, they reported having compensated just 249 survivors of Nazi persecution for male homosexuality (Kingsley 2021). These survivors received 3,000 euros per conviction, plus 1,500 euros for every year of jail time served for homosexuality post-liberation. Still deemed criminals under Paragraph 175, homosexual survivors were sent to prison following the torture and hard labor they endured in their designated camps. This compensation initiative omitted additional restitution for those imprisoned specifically for lesbianism, and there have been no known initiatives to compensate these individuals as of 2024.

Sadly, this initiative concluded in July 2022. Little media coverage existed of this campaign aside from its brief exposure in September 2021. Today, there are countless Americans who have never heard of Nazi persecution and torture of queer individuals. Moreover, the incarceration that awaited the newly freed gay male camp survivors is not in the general consciousness.

On the surface, the horror genre exists to frighten and shock audiences. We forget that the horror genre responds to and reflects disturbing aspects of historical events, often accompanied by fictional depictions and fantastical elements. Unfortunately, the gender/sexual aspects of Nazis in horror have influenced heterosexual and cisgender perceptions of queer people for several decades, perpetuating correlation myths of violence, sinister inclinations, and downright disturbing characterizations. The feminization and queering of Nazis have rendered real queer victims and survivors of Nazi terror invisible by aligning them with one of the world's most disturbing villains. Film theorist Robin Wood extrapolates this point by proclaiming that our patriarchal society "is so reluctant to confront this aspect of Nazism," the forced correlation between Nazism and queerness, because "it has its own stake in the same assumptions" (Picart and Frank 2006, 124). Conservatives now have an arsenal of on-screen queer Nazi portrayals to satiate their malicious appetites for queer destruction, and the horror genre is partly to blame. Furthermore, the existence of transgender Nazis in horror cinema is disturbing for many reasons but mostly due to the lack of transgender representation across all film genres. The fact that within this small minority of trans representation in cinema exist two supposed trans women who identify with the Third Reich results in the continued association with gender non-conformity and fascist ideals. Characters such as the infamous Buffalo Bill and Miss Mann, and the queer Nazis of the Nazisploitation era, complicate the historical narrative of queer victims and survivors and have served only as a perpetuation of cinema's monstrous queer Nazi.

References

American Family Association. "American Family Association." Southern Poverty Law Center, 2022. https://www.splcenter.org/fighting-hate/extremist-files/group/american-family-association

Benshoff, Harry M. *Monsters in the Closet: Homosexuality and the Horror Film.* Manchester: Manchester University Press, 1998.

Dekker, Fred, dir. *The Monster Squad.* DVD. Burbank, CA: Tri-Star Pictures, 2007.

Demme, Jonathan, dir. *The Silence of the Lambs.* DVD. USA: Strong Heart Productions, 2001.

Feder, Sam, dir. *Disclosure.* Los Gatos, CA: Netflix, 2020. https://www.netflix.com/title/81284247

"Ed Gein: Biography, Murderer, Grave Robber, Movies." Biography, 2023. https://www.biography.com/crime/ed-gein

Heger, Heinz. *The Men with the Pink Triangle.* Translated by David Fernbach. London: Gay Men's Press, 1980.

Hoffmann, Heinrich. *Adolf Hitler and his co-conspirators in the 1923 Beer Hall Putsch in Munich.* Photograph, ca. 1924. United States Holocaust Memorial Museum, courtesy of Dottie Bennett.

Holocaust Memorial Day Trust. "Gay People." Accessed August 3, 2023. https://www.hmd.org.uk/learn-about-the-holocaust-and-genocides/nazi-persecution/gay-people/

Holwill, Naomi, dir. *Fascism on a Thread: The Strange Story of Nazisploitation Cinema.* Baton Rouge, LA: High Rising Productions, 2019. https://tubitv.com/movies/565123/fascism-on-a-thread-the-strange-story-of-nazisploitation-cinema

Kasakove, Sophie. "The Fight Over 'Maus' Is Part of a Bigger Cultural Battle in Tennessee." *The New York Times*, March 4, 2022. https://www.nytimes.com/2022/03/04/us/maus-banned-books-tennessee.html

Kingsley, Thomas. "Germany Compensates 249 People Persecuted under Nazi Homosexuality Law." *The Independent*, September 14, 2021. https://www.independent.co.uk/news/world/europe/germany-nazi-homosexuality-law-compensation-b1919795.html

Laguna, Sonny, and Tommy Wiklund, dirs. *Puppet Master: The Littlest Reich.* DVD. Santa Monica, CA: Buffalo 8 Productions et al., 2018.

National Archives and Records Administration. "German students parade in front of the Institute for Sexual Research." Photograph, May 6, 1933. National Archives and Records Administration, College Park, MD. 306-NT-864.

National Archives and Records Administration. "Ilse Koch leaves the courtroom." Photograph, April 16, 1947. National Archives and Records Administration, College Park, MD. 306-NT-864.

Penny, Daniel. "#Milosexual and the Aesthetics of Fascism." *Boston Review,* January 24, 2017. https://www.bostonreview.net/articles/daniel-penny-milosexual/

Picart, Caroline Joan S., and David A. Frank. *Frames of Evil: The Holocaust as Horror in American Film.* Carbondale, IL: Southern Illinois University Press, 2006.

Plant, Richard. *The Pink Triangle: The Nazi War against Homosexuals.* New York: Holt Paperbacks, 1988.

PragerU. "How To Embrace Your Masculinity." 2023. https://www.prageru.com/video/how-to-embrace-your-masculinity

Samberg, Paul, Daniel Wirls, and David Norlin. "Kansans Who Compare COVID-19 Mandates to Holocaust Fuel Antisemitism." *Kansas Reflector,* November 18, 2021. https://kansasreflector.com/2021/11/18/kansans-who-compare-covid-19-mandates-to-holocaust-fuel-antisemitism/

Simic, Olivera. "'No Woman in the Usual Sense': Ilse Koch, the 'Bitch of Buchenwald', Was a Holocaust War Criminal – but Was She Also an Easy Target?" *The Conversation,* September 5, 2023. https://theconversation.com/no-woman-in-the-usual-sense-ilse-koch-the-bitch-of-buchenwald-was-a-holocaust-war-criminal-but-was-she-also-an-easy-target-203960

Singer, Bryan, dir. *Apt Pupil.* VHS. Culver City, CA: SONY Pictures Releasing, 1998.

Smith, Bradley. "Holocaust Denial." Southern Poverty Law Center. Accessed October 31, 2023. https://www.splcenter.org/fighting-hate/extremist-files/ideology/holocaust-denial

Solomon, Haley E., and Beth Kurtz-Costes. "Media's Influence on Perceptions of Trans Women." *Sexuality Research and Social Policy* 15, no. 1 (March 2018): 1-14. https://doi.org/10.1007/s13178-017-0280-2

Visconti, Luchino, dir. *The Damned.* DVD. Italy: Warner Bros. - Seven Arts, 2004.

Wayans, Keenen Ivory, dir. *Scary Movie.* VHS. New York: Dimension Films, 2000.

PART 3:
VERNACULAR
PERSPECTIVES

Chapter Eight
Macho Girl to Poster Girl: Precarious Lives and the Heteronormative Social Order in Himanjali Sankar's *Talking of Muskaan* (2014)

Ashmita Biswas
St. Xavier's College, Kolkata

Abstract

This chapter explores how Himanjali Sankar's *Talking of Muskaan* (2014) initiates an interesting dialogue on the experiences of queer adolescents within the supposedly safe (heteronormative) space of the classroom. As the only existing Young Adult (YA) fiction to delve into the precarious lives of queer youth in India, Sankar's narrative is particularly telling in this regard, as it highlights how the abject lack of gender sensitivity in social institutions is symptomatic of society's deeply embedded heteronormative gender codes. The novel illustrates how belonging and conformity are closely linked, positioning queer children as outliers within the dominant heterosexual matrix. In the young adult fiction that Sankar has so intricately woven, the blatant homophobia of a heteronormative social order is made visible through the othering of Muskaan. Muskaan's social othering from her friend group, peers, and even family is warranted by her inability to conform to accepted gender norms. This study interrogates Muskaan's predicament through the theoretical lens of 'precarity.' The chapter attempts to delve into the social processes of 'girling' and consequently defamiliarize the safety of the classroom by upholding it as an unsafe space for young adults of non-normative sexualities through the trajectory of Muskaan's lived experience as an outed lesbian.

Keywords: Girling, Gender conformity, Heteronormative, Precarity, Homophobia.

***

Introduction

Mehra and Barrett (2021) rightly point out that LGBTQIA+ Young Adult (YA) fiction remains difficult to find in the Indian literary landscape. However, B. J.

Epstein and Elizabeth Chapman, in the introduction to their anthology *International LGBTQ+ Literature for Children and Young Adults* (2021), observe that there has been "little research into how literature written in different countries and different languages and aimed at young people has depicted LGBTQ+ people and issues." While there are countless coming-of-age stories revolving around LGBTQIA+ characters in India, these stories have not been marketed exclusively towards adolescents, but rather intended for readers. Himanjali Sankar's *Talking of Muskaan* (2014) addresses the lack of LGBTQIA+ young adult fiction in India, aiming to raise awareness and foster sensitivity among young readers toward non-normative sexualities. This is a significant gesture in itself since the novel addresses the issue of sexuality, a topic largely neglected within school environments. Over the years, ample research has been conducted in the West to understand how children navigate the murky territories of gender, sex, and sexuality within school and among peer groups without any adult intervention or guidance (Fine 1988; Davies 1989; Thorne 1993; Davies et al. 2001; Halpern 2003; Renold 2004; Moore and Rosenthal 2007; Ali 2010). Past literature suggests that India has seen a growing body of research on children's and adolescents' sexuality (Jejeebhoy 1988; Bansal et al. 2021; Piyali 2021). However, much of this research tends to focus on adolescent reproductive health and well-being, rather than exploring the complex dynamics of peer interactions, an area more commonly addressed in the extensive ethnographic studies conducted in the West.

Past research studies point towards the fact that throughout childhood and adolescence, school goers are exposed to the constitutive processes of 'gendering' that allow little scope for them to go beyond the binarized codes of gender and sexuality. Sankar's fictitious work allows readers to gain insight into the turbulent world of adolescents as they strive to strike a balance between individual identity and social acceptance. This study seeks to examine, through Sankar's novel, how the school serves as a site where identities are continually contested, negotiated, and manipulated through institutionally sanctioned codes of behavior, legitimized by existing social scripts. Fishman wrote: "The point is that in the nineteenth century the control of childhood sexuality became institutionalized" (Fishman 1982, 278). He further observes that children's "normative behaviour" became a "concern of the state," a statement that closely echoes Foucault's (1978) theory of the state's regulation of sexuality as a means of social control. Despite coming from a Western perspective, universally, schools have been proactively involved in normalizing institutionalized heterosexuality.

Conflating sexuality, the state, and social institutions (which also involves the school), Jyoti Puri writes in *Sexual States: Governance and the Struggle Over the Antisodomy Law in India*, "institutions and agencies, spaces, routinized practices, and discourses composing states are thoroughly imbued by considerations of sexuality" (Puri 2016, 6). Added to the never-ending discourse on the entanglements of governance, sexuality, and institutions is children's own understanding of the complex nexus of gender and sexuality: "Children's presumed innocence, sexuality as every day social practice and institutionalized heterosexuality are key themes that punctuate children's own gendered narratives of being a 'girl' and 'boy'" (Renold 2004, 2). The key takeaways from Renold's statement, which form the cornerstone of this paper's engagement with adolescent sexuality, are the emphasis on "everyday social practice" and the focus on "institutionalized heterosexuality."

Talking of Muskaan (2014) gets to the heart of adolescent (hetero)sexual interactions and how that otherizes adolescents of queer/ questioning sexualities as they struggle to fit in. Sayoni Basu, the publisher at Duckbill Books, emphasized the singular nature of the text's contribution: "There are kids who are aware of their sexual orientation early on, and who have difficulty fitting into conventional notions of gender behaviour" (Singh 2014, n.p.). The novel reveals the subcutaneous workings of gendered narratives operating both inside and outside the classroom, in peer groups and as well as the family. The school and peer groups become the sites where "[g]ender dichotomies ('girl/ boy' as basic social categories and as individual identities) provide a continuously available line of difference that can be drawn on at any time in the ongoing life of schools" (Thorne 1993, 35). Gender is indeed an extremely sensitive topic within the school setting. I will offer two anecdotes from my own experience, first as a student in my own school, and then as a teacher interning at an all-boys' school, to demonstrate how insidiously gender dichotomies work.

Back in high school, a friend once made a highly gendered remark about my Avengers pencil case, asking, "Why do you like boys' things?"—implying that interests are inherently tied to one's gender identity. That was in 2014. Fast forward to 2022, and I find myself assigned invigilation duty as a trainee teacher. A tenth-grader comes to the examination hall wearing black nail polish, much to the shock and horror of the teachers present. The moment I caught the boy wearing the nail polish, I had already anticipated that a snarky comment related to his gender deviance would chance upon him, and, my prediction came true when a non-teaching staff, completely disgusted by the fact that a boy is wearing nail polish exclaimed, 'Today he came wearing nail polish, tomorrow he will come wearing lipstick!'

The former comment plays upon stereotypical framings of gender, and the latter is an extension of the former's implications while simultaneously coming across as obliquely queerphobic. The gender politics at work in the latter case is a bit subtle: Instead of commenting on the breach of the school's dress code, the focus is on the boy's penchant for products deemed to belong exclusively to women. Both instances show how the classroom is a breeding ground for the production and reproduction of stereotypical gender binarizations and assumptions, which over time gain legitimacy. This chapter's investigative inquiry will extend beyond a critical discussion of how adolescents respond to and navigate homosexuality, also examining the heteronormative social structures within the classroom that marginalize queer students and render their existence precarious. The following section briefly outlines the analytical framework of the study by tracing the methodologies undertaken in the chapter.

Methodology

As stated in the introduction, there is a concerning lack of both literature and research on the classroom experiences of queer children in India. As an outlier to this tradition, Sankar's novel has raised a significant number of issues that had previously gone unaddressed. In the first section of this chapter, the critical focus is on heteronormativity and its manifestation in the classroom, as illustrated by Sankar through Muskaan's experiences. By narrowing in on research that pointedly analyses the heteronormative social order in the classroom, the section investigates how the invisible yet proactive heterosexual matrix otherizes queer children. By doing so, the study capitalizes on the social pressure faced by queer children to fit into the classroom's heterosexual matrix.

Having established the politics of hegemony informed by heteronormativity in the classroom, the discussion then moves toward examining the figure of the 'school girl' as a subject constructed by social narratives. This logically connects to the section on heteronormativity and otherization, as it exposes the constitutive processes at work that determine who is the ideal subject who would survive in a classroom marked by a heteronormative social order. This section delves into the sharp binarization of identities in the classroom and by drawing particular attention to Muskaan's masculinization by her friends, the section deploys Butler's conceptualization of "girling" (Butler 2004, 177) to out the socialization processes through which one becomes a girl and by extension a subject informed by discourse (Davies et al. 2000).

The last section of the paper invokes Butler's theorization on 'precarity' to underscore the risks surrounding those who do not conform to extant social codes. Precarity and the politics of belonging are closely intertwined, as individuals, particularly in the context of this chapter, who fail to perform gender in accordance with socially sanctioned norms face challenges in establishing a sense of belonging. This is what happens to Muskaan in the text when her friends discover her sexual orientation. Thus, after defamiliarizing the classroom in the first section by dispelling the idea that it is safe for all children, the second section focuses on the ideal school girl who would survive in the classroom as opposed to those, like Muskaan, for whom the same space can become emblematic of a very real threat to her selfhood. Finally, the last section ties together the issues of space and identity with a discussion on precarity and belongingness, thereby offering a holistic understanding of the plight of queer children in Indian classrooms.

Having established the analytical framework of the chapter, it is necessary to acknowledge certain limitations in the chosen methodology. As is evident, there is very little reference to any indigenous theoretical approach in this chapter that might call into question the validity of the research undertaken. However, keeping in mind the danger of an erroneous analysis of Sankar's novel, the Western theoretical frameworks selected have not been applied indiscriminately, but a certain, sure-footed logic is at play. The application of Western scholarship to an Indian text is precarious indeed and runs the risk of having interpretative loopholes, but it isn't something that hasn't been done before. In fact, it is the uncanny similarity of the experiential and situational setting that almost throws the text open to the reception of Western scholarship.

Decoding the Heteronormative Social Order: Is Heterosexuality Compulsory in the Classroom?

Adolescence is considered to be a "critical period" primarily for the "upsurge of sexual drives, the development of sexual values and the initiation of sexual behaviours" (Moore and Rosenthal 2007, 1), making discussions surrounding adolescent sexuality even more crucial. Adolescents are increasingly consciously engaged in constructing their own identities in accordance with the dominant ideologies that shape their interactions. Heteronormativity is the order of the day that dictates how we live. Warner, in the introduction to his edited work *Fear of a Queer Planet: Queer Politics and Social Theory* observed how heteronormative codes are embedded deeply in social institutions: "In the everyday political terrain, contests over sexuality and its regulation are generally linked to views of social institutions and norms of the basic sort" (Warner 1991, xiii). Moore and Rosenthal (2007) identified in their work that "social forces shape adolescents' sexuality by establishing and reestablishing values and norms relating to sexuality and expectations tied to gender" (Moore and Rosenthal 2007, 2). They further highlight:

It has been suggested that sociocultural factors determine how adolescent sexuality is expressed through the cultural context which pervades the adolescents' daily life. Social institutions such as the family and religion exert their influence in three ways: they provide the norms for acceptable sexual behaviour; individuals in powerful roles in these institutions use norms as basis for informal controls; and, finally, there are often formal rules which constrain sexual behaviour through fear of institutional sanctions. (Moore and Rosenthal 2007, 19)

In Sankar's novel, the heteronormative social order orchestrates peer interactions within the classroom as well as outside of it. The close-knit friendship among Muskaan, Aaliya, Divya, Rashika, and Srinjini gradually begins to unravel as Muskaan's growing awareness of her sexual identity clashes with the overtly heterosexual tone that defines the group. The dating culture that surrounds Muskaan is predominantly heterosexual, with all her friends proactively participating in the dating game and also occasionally encouraging Muskaan to engage as well. In this regard, the classroom, a space where heteronormativity is actively advocated and naturalized, becomes a miniature society where a similar play of queer politics can be witnessed. Consequently, Muskaan's lack of interest in the heterosexual dating frenzy is easily taken to be a sign of homosexuality by her classmates, as she sticks out like a sore thumb.

Muskaan's inability to pander to the overbearing heterosexual matrix (Butler 1990) enmeshing her is to be seen in opposition to Aaliya's conscious denial of her own queer identity. Both Muskaan and Aaliya share a deep affection for each other and are aware of their feelings for one another. The difference is that while Muskaan is in full cognizance of her sexual identity, Aaliya deems her love for Muskaan to be irrational. Their attitudes toward validating their sexual orientations become especially evident in the treehouse episode, where Muskaan confides in Aaliya, admitting that she has always known she is gay (Sankar 2014, 38). Aaliya, on the other hand, ventriloquizes the diktat of the heteronormative social order when she says that "life [is] easier when you do what's expected of you" (Sarkar 2014, 36). It is no coincidence that the scene is strategically removed from the classroom. By being removed from the classroom, where heterosexuality is compulsory (Rich 1980), the treehouse functions as a queer heterotopia (Foucault 1967)—a localizable space in which dominant ideologies are "simultaneously represented, contested, and inverted" (Foucault 1967, 17).

Away from the classroom and their girl gang, Muskaan and Aaliya come together, sharing a spontaneous and passionate kiss. But the moment of discovery is broken when Aaliya promptly declares that she's not gay, and keeps trying to defend heterosexuality as the natural sexual order with procreative functionality (Sarkar 2014, 38). Aaliya is under the influence of what Ingraham (1994) theorized as the "heterosexual imaginary," which is "that way of thinking which conceals the operation of heterosexuality in structuring gender and closes off any critical analysis of heterosexuality as an organizing institution" (Ingraham 1994, 203-204). Muskaan's cry for help falls on deaf ears as Aaliya fails to grasp the deep psychological crisis behind her drowning metaphor: "It's like I'm…underwater all the time…without my oxygen tank. And all of you are on the boat having a party" (Sarkar 2014, 40). Outwardly, Aaliya is reluctant to reciprocate Muskaan's feelings, but inwardly she is aware of her attraction towards her: "Muskaan and I had always been special […] I loved Muskaan more than any other friend. Always have. It was alright. Love is strange. It just happened. And it was something awesome. It couldn't be wrong. Ever" (Sarkar 2014, 41).

Muskaan is severely bullied once her classmates get wind of the fact that she's a lesbian, cued by her romantic disinterest in boys (Sarkar 2014, 59). Her supposed homosexuality becomes the topic of gossip and speculation, and she keeps growing distant from her girl gang. Several disparaging terms are thrown around, like "weirdo," "homo," "freak," and "abnormal," which mark her outsider status within the heterosexual matrix of the classroom. She becomes the butt of jokes in the school bus as students crack "gay jokes" and two girls mime kissing while the boys hoot and clap (Sarkar 2014, 107). When her girl gang hears of Muskaan being bullied, none of them step in to help her, and Aaliya, Muskaan's love interest, is perhaps the cruelest. She deliberately avoids Muskaan after the tree house incident, and believes that Muskaan must "learn to look after herself" (Sarkar 2014, 66) while dealing with bullies.

Aaliya is a queer masquerading as straight to blend in with the classroom's heteronormative social order to the extent that she goes out of her way to initiate a heterosexual encounter: "I was glad I'd kissed a boy at last. I didn't want to be lesbian or even bisexual. Everyone made fun of gays" (Sarkar 2014, 66). While Muskaan doesn't deny her homosexuality, Aaliya is afraid of even acknowledging her bisexuality, lest she is ostracized by her peers. Aaliya, thus, becomes a case in point illustrating how the heteronormative social order heterosexualizes subjects through its exclusionary politics.

"Macho Girl to Poster Girl": The School Girl As A Subject

Muskaan is the locus of all negative attention from friends, peers, and even her own family, simply because she does not fit in. One of the central concerns of girlhood studies is the process of "girling" (Butler 2004, 177), which refers to the socialization processes through which one becomes a girl. This section of the paper will read into the representation of the school girl as a subject who "simultaneously constitutes herself and is constituted through discourse" (Davies et al. 2001). From the Butlerian standpoint, "the political construction of the subject proceeds with certain legitimating and exclusionary aims, and these political operations are effectively concealed and naturalized by a political analysis that takes juridical structures as their foundation" (Butler 1990, 3). By definition, then, Muskaan isn't the ideal school girl subject since, as a lesbian, she stands outside the heteronormative social order.

Girling as a constitutive process of feminization continues well into adolescence. Sankar's novel illustrates how the process is at work by drawing attention to how Muskaan becomes her gang's feminization project. Muskaan's failure to entertain herself with 'girly' affairs invites unfavorable remarks about her gender deviance. In what I have labeled as the waxing episode, Muskaan's friends make a fuss about waxing her arms, and Divya articulates Muskaan's feminization will be deemed complete after waxing—"Macho Girl to Poster Girl" (Sarkar 2014, 14)—with each representative image of girlhood positioned at extreme opposite ends of the spectrum. Muskaan's masculinization is prompted by her refusal to wax and don flowery dresses, contrasted with the "Poster Girl," which is the ultimate image of ideal femininity. Aaliya further taunts her by calling her "Macho Musko" (Sarkar 2014, 17) and saying that she has an attractive masculine charm (Sarkar 2014, 17).

That masculinity and femininity can only exist in opposition to each other is reified by Muskaan's blatant masculinization. Muskaan becomes an outlier to the heteronormative gender binarizations, and her gender deviance eventually leads people to believe that she is sexually deviant as well. It is Lucal who posited that "sexual deviance is assumed to be signalled by gender deviance, just as sexual conformity is assumed to be evidenced by gender conformity" (2008). Muskaan fits into the stereotype of the "tomboy," a term used to describe girls who possess masculine traits, which is considered to be a gender "deviance" (Thorne 1993, 111). As opposed to Muskaan's lack of femininity, which isolates her from her group, the girls' waxing ritual, especially in Srinjini's case, who is looking forward to being complimented by her boyfriend Imran on her freshly waxed arms, problematizes the adolescent female's self-image. Ali notes how femininity is tied to "bodily practices and these often revolve around desirability to the opposite sex" (Ali 2010, 278). It is not simply as casual as "something that girls do" (Sarkar 2014, 17) like Divya says, rather this "sexualized cosmetic culture" that defines the rites of passage to ideal femininity internalized by female adolescents panders to the male gaze (Holland et al. 1998), and reveals how adolescent female sexuality is informed by external forces like "peers," "culture," and "body" to name a few (Espin 1984; Omolade 1983, cited by Fine 1988, 35).

Muskaan consciously resists being subjected to the girls' attempts to mold her a certain way. She complains to Aalia: "You guys treat me like this kid gone astray who just needs to be beaten into shape" (Sarkar 2014, 40). Her inability to fit in draws the other students', especially the boys', attention. Prateek initially found her to be beautiful (Sarkar 2014, 22), but after she turns down his proposal, he finds her to be strange, a "weirdo" (Sarkar 2014, 48), and his friends call her a "psycho" (Sarkar 2014, 49). Even Shubhojoy finds her to be a bit "strange" (Sarkar 2014, 46). However, while Muskaan never resists being disparagingly called out for her alterity, Aaliya remains afraid of being outed. Aaliya is going through a phase where she is trying to ascertain whether her love for Muskaan is a solitary incident or whether she is really bisexual. This phase is an essential phase for adolescents: "Crucial for adolescents is the distinction between transitory same-sex sexual acts and homosexual identification" (Moore and Rosenthal 2007, 123). Slowly but surely, the reality of her sexual orientation dawns on Aaliya:

> It was, like gender didn't matter to me – it was the person. I could equally well be attracted to a boy or a girl. But I plan to condition my mind to be attracted to boys only. Surely I could do that. I could let the boy attractions grow and the girl ones I could ignore. It would make life that much easier if I could just do that. (Sarkar 2014, 100)

Sankar's problematization of the school girl as a subject is made amply evident through the ways in which Muskaan is perennially pushed to the margins. Muskaan resists the internalization of gendered discourses surrounding the schoolgirl and emerges as an isolated case of the schoolgirl as a failed subject, a position that renders her existence precarious. "The very possibility of a 'lived life' depends on being recognized as a legitimate and legible subject" (Varela and Dhawan 2011, 95-96). The following section of the paper tackles the intersectionality of gender performativity, livability and precarity as made evident by Muskaan's plight.

Precarious Lives and the Politics of Belonging

Butler theorized extensively on the state of 'precarity,' postulating that "we continue to live in a world in which one can risk serious disenfranchisement and physical violence for the pleasure one seeks, the fantasy one embodies, the gender one performs" (Butler 2004, 214). Of particular interest to this paper is how Butler ties together the conceptual framework of precarity with gender performativity and sexuality, stating that precarity is "directly linked with gender norms, since we know that those who do not live their genders in intelligible ways are at heightened risk for harassment and violence" (Butler 2009, ii). The idea is that whether one performs gender as per the socially sanctioned codes or not determines "who will count as a subject, and who will not" (Butler 2009, iv): "The performativity of gender has everything to do with who counts as a life, who can be read or understood as a living being, and who lives, or tries to live, on the far side of established modes of intelligibility" (Butler 2009, iv).

Sankar's text opens up a discussion on the precarity of queer lives as it depicts the re-criminalization of homosexuality in India that took place in 2014 when the Supreme Court overturned the ruling of NAZ Foundation v. Govt. of NCT of Delhi (2009) which had decreed that treating homosexuality as a crime is a violation of the fundamental rights guaranteed by the Indian Constitution.[1] The novel shows fifteen-year-old Muskaan's world turning topsy-turvy as she is abandoned by friends and family since no one around her shares favorable views about her sexuality. The climate of fear intensifies with the re-criminalization verdict as the fifteen-year-old's very existence is marked as nature's aberration, and her identity is criminalized. Warner had rightly surmised that it is queer youths who are the most vulnerable: "Heterosexual ideology, in combination with a potent ideology about gender and identity in maturation, therefore bears down in the heaviest and often deadliest way on those with the least resources to combat: queer children and teens" (Warner 1993, xvi).

Muskaan is continually politically positioned on the fringes, barely seeking any interaction. While her girl group does reach out to her, they are reluctant to discuss her homosexuality or to provide a safe and non-judgmental space. The narrative also shows how people perceive homosexuals in a predominantly negative light, often subscribing to the idea that their entire act is just to seek attention. Prateek's father holds this belief and actively encourages his son to participate in homophobic behavior. His father also propagates the notion that homosexuals are different and a danger to society. Prateek and his father's conversations on homosexuality influence his attitude towards Muskaan a great deal. He begins to villainize Muskaan and holds her accountable for all the misfortune that has befallen him lately, wielding a conspiracy theory that she is getting back at him because she's jealous of his relationship with Rashika and regrets turning down his proposal.

Muskaan is violently outed before the entire class as Prateek decides to punish her for allegedly conspiring against him, as he calls her "abnormal" on account of being a homosexual (Sarkar 2014, 114). He even rationalizes his act in his own head by using the law as his aid, knowing that "not only [him] but the laws of the country didn't support people like [Muskaan]" (Sarkar 2014, 121). It is the faulty law that enables homophobes like Prateek to continue battering queers verbally, psychologically, and physically, and Sankar has deftly shown how homophobia operates within the classroom. Jyoti Puri commented on how discourses on sexuality can deeply impact discourses on normality, bodies, and people: "sexuality impacts states just as much as states seek to define sexual normality, discipline bodies, and control populations" (Puri 2004, 11).

Muskaan has been so severely bullied and left out that even she regrets being a lesbian. She is almost envious of straight people, and she considers her friend

---

[1] https://en.wikipedia.org/wiki/Naz_Foundation_v._Govt._of_NCT_of_Delhi

Shubhojoy lucky because he is "straight" like "normal" people – the one "luxury" that she doesn't have (Sarkar 2014, 80). Shubhojoy is yet another character who, like Muskaan, doesn't belong to the mainstream group of students. At one point, he reflects on belonging to the "margins" (Sarkar 2014, 84). Shubhojoy's inability to belong is due to his economic condition, which is significantly worse compared to that of students from affluent families. It is Shubhojoy's outsider status that allows him to get close to Muskaan, and he becomes the second person, after Aaliya, before whom she willingly comes out.

It is Aaliya who raises the question of 'belongingness' when she ponders over her parents' ability to truly understand the plight of queer people who were now being forced to go back into their closets after the 2014 verdict. She goes over the fact that, though both her parents were supportive of the LGBT+ community, they both "belonged" and were thus politically protected. From such a position of safety, "it is elegant and nice to ask interesting questions", but what if they didn't belong, like Aaliya and Muskaan: "Then did you rave and rant at society? Or did you just wish you belonged?" (Sarkar 2014, 135). Aaliya's thoughts reflect her own dilemma as well – should she come out to her friends and family and as a result become a precarious subject? Or, should she continue staying in the closet, masquerade as a straight person, and hence keep belonging to mainstream society? It is she who reminds Muskaan that she is a "criminal" (Sarkar 2014, 138), after which Muskaan, unable to bear society's diatribes, downs a handful of pills to end it all. Aaliya does come out, but it takes Muskaan a suicide attempt followed by a miraculous survival and recovery for Aaliya to submit herself to her true sexual identity.

Critical Reflections and Impact on Indian Educational Policies and Pedagogies

By way of conclusion, it is necessary to vindicate the significance of Sankar's text in a real-world setting by relating it to similar issues faced by children of nonnormative sexual identities in Indian educational institutions. Nisha Kapoor, in her article "Faltering Attempts to Increase Inclusivity in Indian Schools" (2022), highlights the NCERT's recognition of transgender children in schools through a draft manual, which was significant but was later withdrawn, and sadly, no further steps have been taken to make the classroom gender-inclusive. By interviewing a couple of school children, Nitika, in her article "Section 377 is gone, but schools are stuck in the British era" (2022), delves deep into the homophobic bullying experienced by them. In a blog post titled "*School Policies on Gender and Sexuality*" (2022), Nayantara Narayanan cites a study conducted by UNESCO's New Delhi office, which revealed that among 371 gay and transgender men and women between 18 and 22 experienced bullying and sexual harassment in primary school. Research on homophobic bullying encountered by school students is scant but not completely absent.

Dr Zaid Al Baset (2023), in his article titled "*For that sliver of hope*," published in 'Varta' Webzine, vocalized the practice of inclusion in educational institutions as the need of the hour. In the article, the author invokes the precarious position accorded to people of nonnormative sexual identities, given the uncertain history of criminalization, decriminalization, and re-criminalization of same-sex relations in India. Drawing attention to the National Education Policy's statement on inclusivity in schools in 2020, Baset notes how this attempt at inclusivity, intended to bridge the social gaps that socio-economically disadvantaged groups (SEDGs) experience, omits taking into account those marginalized on the basis of their sexual orientation. The complete erasure of the terms 'sexuality' and 'sexual orientation,' according to Baset, is a "classic instance of the heteronormativity of the State." Baset's article also emphasizes how acknowledgement and validation in the classroom can "engender a hope to survive outside it, and sometimes, it is survival that is at stake."

Given the real-world debates and discussions surrounding the overt and covert forms of homophobic bullying and victimization faced by queer children/adolescents, Sankar's text is reparative in the sense that it tries to break the silence surrounding the issue. Instead of viewing the chapter's focused exploration of the text as a limitation, the nuanced forms of homophobic bullying shown in the narrative prove to be educational for readers. Arriving at the question of whether the text can potentially impact educational policies and foster real-world changes would lead one to examine the history of India's struggle with not only legitimizing but also truly acknowledging the rights of its queer population. While laws and policies are significant and necessary for sexual citizenship, the real change and acceptance need to come from people's mindset, and Sankar's text strikes a dexterous balance between the two.

Conclusion: Queering the Classroom

The paper thus establishes the significance of prioritizing, recognizing, and acknowledging adolescents with nonnormative sexualities. The classroom needs to be a safe, inclusive, and non-judgmental space where queer children will not be stigmatized for not meeting the markers of normative gender performativity and for being different from the other students. The paper arrives at such a conclusion by illustrating how childhood (especially girlhood in this case) and adolescence are social constructs and by simultaneously exposing the school as a "social and cultural arena" that produces and reproduces gender and sexual identities (Haywood and Mac and Ghaill 1995, 1996; Laskey and Beavis 1996; Kehily 2002; Epstein et al. 2003, cited in Renold

(2004). Renold (2004, 9) rightly points out that the queering of childhood sensitizes people towards the "(hetero)gendered and (hetero)sexualized nature of identity categories such as 'girl,' 'boy' and 'child' and foregrounds the heteronormativity of children's childhoods more widely." In other words, queer theory reveals the often hidden dynamics of sexual politics within the school setting. Such complexities warrant the need to "understand and theorize young people's sexuality in all its diversity" (Halpern 2003, 1).

Davies (1989) makes the following case: "The child is not a passive receptacle of the socialization process, rather an active agent partaking in the meaning-making process – in processes of gendering and actively contribute/ contrive, construct and maintain their social and cultural worlds." Children's, and by extension, adolescents' sexuality is a taboo topic, but it should not necessarily be so. Foucault discussed the "pedagogization of children's sex" (Foucault 1978, 104) where he posited that children's sexual nature has been rigorously regulated and obscured by authorities under the guise of "presumed innocence" (Fishman 1982, 20), while Raphaela Best (1983) averred that children engage in their own sexual learning via the third hidden curriculum, which takes place unbeknownst to the adults surrounding them. As such, talks regarding sex and sexuality education at all stages of school become imperative in order to lift the "fictional fabrics of 'proper' school and university practices" (Walkerdine 1997, 168), making the classroom more inclusive.

References

Ali, Suki. "'To Be a Girl': Culture and Class in Schools Correspondence : Suki Ali, Goldsmiths College, University of London, Sociology Department, New Cross, London SE14 6NW, UK. E-Mail: S.Ali@gold.Ac.Uk." *Gender and Education* 15 (3), 2023: 269–83. https://doi.org/10.1080/09540250303859

Baset, Zaid Al. "For That Sliver of Hope | Varta Trust." Varta Trust. August 23, 2023. https://vartagensex.org/2023/08/30/for-that-sliver-of-hope/

Best, Raphaela. *We've All Got Scars: What Boys and Girls Learn in Elementary School.* Indiana University Press. 1989.

Butler, Judith. *Gender Trouble: Feminism and the Subversion of Identity.* Routledge. 1990.

---. *Undoing Gender.* Psychology Press. 2004.

---. "Performativity, Precarity and Sexual Politics." Lecture, Universidad Complutense de Madrid, Madrid. 2009.

Davies, Bronwyn. "The Discursive Production of the Male/Female Dualism in School Settings." *Oxford Review of Education* 15 (3), 1989: 229–41. https://doi.org/10.1080/0305498890150304

Davies, Bronwyn, Suzy Dormer, Sue Gannon, Cath Laws, Sharn Rocco, Hillevi Lenz Taguchi, and Helen McCann. "Becoming Schoolgirls: The Ambivalent Project of Subjectification." *Gender and Education* 13 (2), 2001: 167–82. https://doi.org/10.1080/09540250124848

Epstein, B. J., and Elizabeth Chapman. *International LGBTQ+ Literature for Children and Young Adults.* Anthem Press. 2021. https://doi.org/10.2307/j.ctv1zvccfh

Fine, Michelle. "Sexuality, Schooling, and Adolescent Females: The Missing Discourse of Desire." *Harvard Educational Review* 58 (1), 1988: 29–54. https://doi.org/10.17763/haer.58.1.u0468k1v2n2n8242

Fishman, Sterling. "The History of Childhood Sexuality." *Journal of Contemporary History* 17 (2), 1982: 269–83. https://doi.org/10.1177/002200948201700204

Foucault, Michel. *The History of Sexuality: An Introduction.* Vintage. 1990.

Halpern, C. T. "Biological influences on adolescent romantic and sexual behavior." In *Adolescent Romantic and Sexual Behavior: Theory, Research and Practical Implications,* edited by P. Florsheim. 57-84. Lawrence Erlbaum Associates Publishers. 2003.

Holland, Janet. *The Male in the Head: Young People, Heterosexuality and Power.* The Tufnell Press. 1998.

Ingraham, Chrys. "The Heterosexual Imaginary: Feminist Sociology and Theories of Gender." *Sociological Theory* 12 (2), 1994: 203. https://doi.org/10.2307/201865

K, Nitika. "Section 377 Is Gone, but Schools Are Stuck in the British Era – The Softcopy." February 24, 2022. https://thesoftcopy.in/2022/02/24/section-377-is-gone-but-schools-are-stuck-in-the-british-era/

Kapoor, Nishka. "Faltering Attempts To Increase Inclusivity In Indian Schools — Human Rights Pulse." Human Rights Pulse. January 17, 2022. https://www.humanrightspulse.com/mastercontentblog/faltering-attempts-to-increase-inclusivity-in-indian-schools

Lucal, Betsy. "Teaching and Learning Guide for: Building Boxes and Policing Boundaries: (De)Constructing Intersexuality, Transgender and Bisexuality." *Sociology Compass* 2 (2), 2008: 792–98. https://doi.org/10.1111/j.1751-9020.2008.00100.x

Mehra, Bharat and Christ Barrett. "Out of the Closet? Exploring the Infoscape of LGBTQ+ Fiction For / About Youth in India." In *International LGBTQ+ Literature for Children and Young Adults,* edited by B. J. Epstein and Elizabeth Chapman. Anthem Press. 2021. https://doi.org/10.2307/j.ctv1zvccfh.11

Moore, Susan, Doreen Rosenthal, Susan M. Moore, and Doreen A. Rosenthal. *Sexuality in Adolescence: Current Trends.* Routledge. 2007. https://doi.org/10.4324/9780203695036

Narayanan, Nayantara. "School Policies on Gender and Sexuality - Centre for Law & Policy Research." Centre for Law & Policy Research. August 16, 2022. https://clpr.org.in/blog/school-policies-on-gender-and-sexuality/#:~:text=A%20study%20by%20UNESCO'S%20New,school%20due%20to%20their%20queerness

Puri, Jyoti. *Sexual States: Governance and the Struggle over the Antisodomy Law in India.* Duke University Press. 2016. https://doi.org/10.1515/9781478091257

Renold, Emma. *Girls, Boys, and Junior Sexualities: Exploring Children's Gender and Sexual Relations in the Primary School.* Routledge. 2005. https://doi.org/10.4324/9780203561584

Rich, Adrienne Cecile. "Compulsory Heterosexuality and Lesbian Existence (1980)." *Journal of Women's History* 15 (3), 2003: 11–48. https://doi.org/10.1353/jowh.2003.0079

Sankar, Himanjali. *Talking of Muskaan.* Penguin Random House India Private Limited. 2014.

Singh, Preeti. "Are India's Young Adults Ready for LGBT Literature?" *midday.com: Culture News*, 3 December, 2014. https://www.mid-day.com/lifestyle/culture/article/Are-India-s-young-adults-ready-for-LGBT-literature--15810191

Thorne, Barrie. *Gender Play: Girls and Boys in School.* Rutgers University Press. 1993.

Varela, María Do Mar Castro, Nikita Dhawan, and Antke Engel. *Hegemony and Heteronormativity: Revisiting "the Political" in Queer Politics.* Ashgate Publishing Company. 2011.

Walkerdine, Valerie. *Daddy's Girl: Young Girls and Popular Culture.* Harvard University Press. 1998.

Warner, Michael. *Fear of a Queer Planet: Queer Politics and Social Theory.* U of Minnesota Press. 1993.

Contributors

Dhishna Pannikot is an Associate Professor in English in the School of Social Sciences & Management, National Institute of Technology Karnataka. She specializes in travel writing, cultural studies, gender studies and comparative literature. She completed her MA, MPhil, and PhD at Pondicherry Central University and won the gold medal for the Best Meritorious PhD in 2010. She won the Venus International Foundation award, "Young Woman in Language Studies," for her contribution to and achievement in the field of English Language in 2017. She has widely travelled to countries including Sri Lanka, Malaysia, and Indonesia to give talks at conferences and present papers. She won the best paper award at the IEDRC conference in Bali, Indonesia, in 2016. She is guiding ten research scholars in multidisciplinary areas of literature. She is a member of professional bodies including the Indian Association for Women's Studies, ASLE India, the International Economics Development Research Centre, and the Indian Association for Commonwealth Literature and Language Studies (IACLALS). She had served as a resource person at numerous national and international conferences in India and abroad. She has published a book on "Outcome Based Education: Towards a Pedagogic Shift" in 2016. She has published in various national and international journals, including Scopus publications.

Tanupriya is an Assistant Professor with the Department of English and Cultural Studies, CHRIST (Deemed to be University), Delhi NCR campus. She is an awarded gold medalist for her MPhil English. She was awarded a JASSO (Japan Student Services Organization) fellowship for attending a conference at Kumamoto University, Kumamoto, Japan. She has published her works in various peer-reviewed Scopus-indexed journals. Her book chapters are published with Springer, Temple University Press, Routledge and Palgrave Macmillan. She is an editorial board member for the Routledge Handbook of Descriptive Rhetorical Studies and World Languages. Her research interests are Queer visual culture, Female and Queer Body Image, Trans sexualities and writing the self, and varied aspects related to frameworks of gender and sexuality.

Abigail Waldron is a historian who specializes in queer and film history, particularly the horror genre. She is the author of *Queer Screams: A History of LGBTQ+ Survival Through the Lens of American Horror Cinema* (2022), a contributing writer for Horror Press, and has been published in *Hear Us Scream: The Voices of Horror*, Volume II (2022).

Ashmita Biswas is a Research Scholar at the Department of English, St. Xavier's College (Autonomous), Kolkata. She has presented her papers at several National and International Seminars, and has a few publications to her credit. Her areas of interest include Queer Studies, Gender and Sexuality, Indian Writing in English, Memory studies, Popular Culture & Manga studies. She is currently working as a Faculty (Visiting) at the Department of English, The Neotia University.

Avijit Pramanik is Assistant Professor of English and Head, Department of Basic Sciences; Humanities, Ramkrishna Mahato Government Engineering College, Purulia, West Bengal, India. His research interests include Disability Studies, American Literature, and Soft Skills. He has published in *Asiatic, Rupkatha, The IUP Journal of English Studies, Postcolonial Text, South Asia Research, Littcrit*, and many other journals.

Ayse Irem Karabag (she/they) is in their second year of the PhD program in English Studies at York University, Toronto. Their research focuses on queer refugee worldmaking in contemporary literature across the world and the connection between literature, protest, borders and migration. Prior to arriving at York, Irem completed their Master's degree in English and Transcultural Studies at the University of Heidelberg, Germany. Their MA thesis focused on the "slacking" practices of white-collar workers in contemporary American literature. In 2017, they received their BA from Bogazici University, Istanbul.

Dhananjay Tripathi acquired his MA (2006) and D.Phil. (2013) in English from the University of Allahabad, India, and he is an Associate Professor and Head of Department and Research Supervisor in the Department of Humanities and Social Sciences at the National Institute of Technology Sikkim, India.

Iraboty Kazi (she/her) is a Bangladeshi Canadian scholar who received her PhD in Art and Visual Culture at the University of Western Ontario in 2025. Her dissertation explored the ways the spaces presented in Italian Early Modern pastoral paintings are reconfigured and mobilized in constructions of nature in contemporary queer cinema. Her recent publications include "A Living Colour of Light: Yvonne Williams and the Art of Stained Glass" and "Almost Heaven: *Call Me by Your Name* as a Queer Earthly Paradise."

Kayla Reed is an Assistant Professor at Grinnell College, United States. Kayla Reed's research and teaching focus on diversity and LGBTQ+ issues, with a focus on Asexuality, intersection, and cooperation of library departments, as well as emotional labor in the workforce.

Sandra Jacobo is a recent graduate of the University of Kansas (2024) and currently serves as a Just Transformations Postdoctoral Scholar at Penn State University. Her research meets at the intersection of Caribbean literature, Black Feminisms, Queer Studies and Popular Culture. Besides fulfilling the dreams of her ancestors, Dr. Jacobo is invested in creating scholarship that celebrates the nuances of Black women and femme experiences.

Sanjana Chakraborty acquired her Bachelors (2016) and Masters (2018) of Arts in English from Banaras Hindu University, India, UGC-NET (2019), and is a Research Scholar in the Department of Humanities and Social Sciences at the National Institute of Technology Sikkim, India. Her area of research interest is Gender Studies, Masculinity Studies, Literature, Gender-Based Violence, and South Asian Studies.

www.ingramcontent.com/pod-product-compliance
Lightning Source LLC
Chambersburg PA
CBHW050523280326
41932CB00014B/2433